Painting & Wallpapering

BY LEANNA LANDSMANN

GROSSET
GOOD LIFE
BOOKS

PUBLISHERS • GROSSET & DUNLAP • NEW YORK

Acknowledgments

Produced for Grosset & Dunlap by Media Projects Inc., New York, N.Y.
Cover photograph by Mort Engel
Illustrations by Sara Stein
Photographs by John Marmarus

Instructions and safety precautions in this book have been carefully checked for accuracy. However, the author and publisher do not warrant or guarantee results and cannot be responsible for any adverse consequences resulting from the use of information contained herein. The author has attempted to assist the reader in avoiding problems by setting forth appropriate and recommended procedures.

Contents

1
Painting

Most do-it-yourself home decorators like to paint. The process is simple, results are immediate, and anyone can do a good job no matter how few hours logged with brush in hand.

Painting is a fast way to decorate. Spend an afternoon with a roller and a brush and you can give any room in your house a new look by evening. Painting is also the least expensive way to finish the interior of your home. For pinched budgets and tight schedules, nothing beats it.

Paint manufacturers have had non-professionals in mind as they introduced new lines in recent years. Gone are the smelly, hard-to-spread, easy-to-streak, drip-prone varieties that made amateurs shy away from home painting. It's easy to find a paint that's right for every surface you have to cover — wood, metal, concrete, or plaster.

Clean-up is no longer a trauma with water-base paints. New types of brushes, rollers and daubers do much to simplify the job at less cost than before.

Painting projects can also be family projects — young children excepted. There are easy tasks such as large surfaces and more difficult tasks such as doors and trim in every room, so two or three people with varying skills can work together to get the job done more quickly.

Throughout this book we describe procedures and methods most commonly recommended by professionals while offering short-cuts along with accepted ways, suggesting substitutes for traditional equipment, and encouraging you to work at your own pace and be inventive in solving problems that might pop up.

Everyone works differently. And in this book, we tip our hat to individual differences in work habits. Some of you are methodical workers who want to take the right steps and proper precautions and acquire the recommended equipment to guarantee just the results you want. Some of you prefer to take the short cuts, make do with a self-engineered piece of equipment (because you know you can), opt for risk to save a bit of time — and get just the results you want. That's the joy of painting. You can suit it to your personality, your temperament, your family's schedule, your free time, and then, when it's all done, what a wonderful difference it makes!

Choosing A Color

Choosing colors can be one of the most exciting parts of any painting project — or one of the most frustrating. Trying to visualize the effect of a small sample from a color chart is difficult without some basic facts about color.

Colors can set a mood: you know yellow perks up some people, drives others up a wall. Greens calm some of us, leave others with the chills. Reds, some doctors say, increase blood pressure and promote activity. Blues, according to research, slow down breathing and decrease muscular tension. Grey and beige, the "neutral" colors are loved or hated for their lack of emphasis. Yellow, peach, and rose tones are thought by some to stimulate the appetite making them dining room favorites. Purple tones rank high as a bathroom choice but low in other parts of the house.

Color acceptance is often a matter of conditioning. You know best what certain colors do (or don't do) for your psyche. Create a color mood based on what *you like* not on what a dealer or decorating consultant thinks you should have.

Colors, most agree, can make you feel cool or warm. In a room that gets full sun, a bright orange or yellow might be too much. They might be perfect though for a room with a northern exposure. Likewise, a green or blue might be right for the sunny room, but unsatisfactory for the room with little direct light. Experiment by hanging fabric swatches (or towels or blankets) to see the effect exposure has on certain colors.

Colors can emphasize or obscure the features of a room. Used to advantage this is called "paint styling." If you want to set off an alcove or a particular group of furniture, paint the background a color that compliments the rest of the room. The back walls of book shelves might be painted to match the dominant tone in the wallpaper elsewhere in the room. Some moldings and trim can be painted to make them "outline" a room if it has a shape you want to emphasize. A high ceiling can be lowered by painting it a darker color than the walls; paint a low ceiling white to raise it.

Conversely, to obscure such features as moldings, pipes and radiators, paint them the same color as the rest of the room, or pick up the background tone if you're wall papering.

Invest in and apply a small quantity of a color if you aren't sure you'll like it. If you don't you'll start again, knowing you've prevented a decorating goof you would have had to live with. If the paint isn't quite the right color, you can use it up on odd jobs such as inside cupboards, drawers or toy chests.

Look at your paint choice in both artificial and natural lighting; also check it against the carpet or floor color, curtains, bedspread, furniture coverings, picture frames, and other elements which will influence the look of the room. When you go to the store to pick out your paint, take curtain, upholstery, wallpaper and carpet samples with you if possible. Beware of the effect of fluorescent lighting in most stores, however. It is harsher and bluer than the incandescent lighting you probably have at home, and will distort the colors you are looking at. Another caution: Paint chips can often be deceptive because they are so small. Most tones will look darker on the wall, or bolder and brighter. Beige tones may look neutral in the store, but quite pink or too yellow on the wall. Paint chips that have been around for a while may even have faded.

Experiment as much as possible if you are in a color quandry: hold up solid color fabric or paper to help visualize the effect of basic color combinations. If you feel that color samples provided by the paint manufacturer are inadequate, buy and try a small quantity.

Using fabric swatches and paint chip samples from a paint store, experiment with various color combinations. If you are undecided take a couple of days to come to a decision. Look at the samples under night and day lighting, check them against other room elements such as curtains and carpets and even consider their effect, if any, on your moods.

Estimating Quantity

Estimating the paint required is a simple measuring job. If you don't have a yardstick or tape measure use one of the fabric tape measures that come in sewing kits. Though going around corners will be easier with the fabric type, they are difficult to use single handedly. Don't use a 12-inch school ruler — it's too easy to lose count in all that moving from place to place. Find the square feet of wall area to be covered by measuring the room's perimeter (the distance around) and multiply the perimeter by the room's height. Deduct areas in square feet that you won't be painting such as fireplaces or papered alcoves. Don't deduct windows unless their total area exceeds 100 square feet. If you plan to use a different type of paint on bookshelves or cabinets deduct those areas too. To determine how many gallons or quarts you'll need, divide the remaining area by the number of square feet per gallon the paint will cover. (This information is usually on the label. If not, ask your dealer.) For example, let's say you have a room that is 12 feet wide and 16 feet long with walls 8 feet high. Find the perimeter: 12 + 16 + 12 + 16 = 56. Multiply it by ceiling height: 56 × 8 = 448 square feet. A gallon of paint, which is said to cover 500 square feet, will give you enough for one coat.

For ceilings and floors, multiply width times length to obtain area in square feet; divide, as above, by the expected square feet per gallon.

If you plan to use a different paint for trim, woodwork and bookshelves, there's no pat formula for estimating. Figure roughly the square feet to be covered and combine your own judgement with your dealer's experience. If there's a minimum amount to be painted, start with a quart and go back for another if necessary. If you think you'll need 3-4 quarts, buy a gallon since it's usually as cheap (sometimes cheaper) than buying 3 quarts separately. If you're going to need two coats, remember that the second will probably take less paint than the first.

If the walls being painted are particularly porous, you may need more for the first coat than the formula indicates.

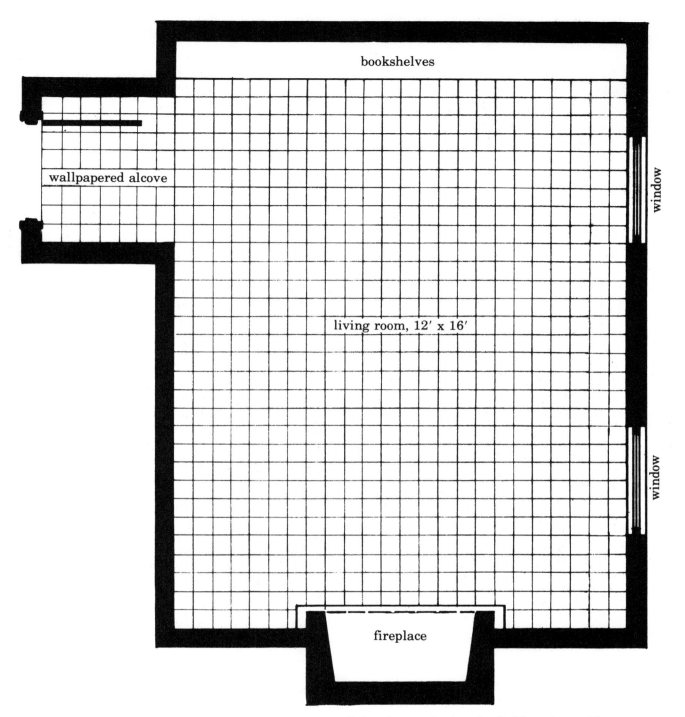

bookshelves

wallpapered alcove

window

living room, 12' x 16'

window

fireplace

To know how much paint to buy find the perimeter of the room and multiply it by the height, which gives roughly the area in square feet to be covered. Use this for figuring each coat: primer, first coat, and second coat if necessary. In this room don't deduct for the windows since they are small and their total area does not exceed 100 square feet. If flat latex is to be used for the walls and a matching enamel semi-gloss is to be used for the book-shelves, deduct the large book-shelf area when figuring the quantity of latex needed.

Types Of Paint

Types of paints and varnishes are categorized by the solvents that are used to thin them. There are two basic paint categories: oil base (thinned by a turpentine-related solvent) and water base (thinned with water). Both come in three finishes: flat, semi-gloss, and full or high gloss. In addition, there is sometimes an intermediate finish called "satin," which is slightly less shiny than semi-gloss.

Remember this simple rule of thumb: flat paints are best on walls or ceilings. High or semi-gloss finishes work best on doors, windows, woodwork and trim. The paint and finish you buy will depend on the areas to be covered.

Water Base Paints

Latex paints, which are the only water base paints used these days, spread easily, dry in less than two hours, and have little odor. Clean-up of brushes, hands, clothes and spattered areas is a snap with soap and water.

Latex primer-sealer is needed if you need to prime wallboard, plaster, or wood walls or ceilings. Priming is usually only necessary when a surface is painted for the first time. It goes on easily and dries fast. One coat is usually enough unless the surface is extremely porous — in that case, count on adding a second.

Flat latex wall paint, the most important innovation for the do-it-yourselfer, can be used on all primed drywall, plaster, wallboard and new masonry. It too covers easily, is fast drying, can be touched up and does not leave brush or lap marks. It is nontoxic and has very little odor. Most are also nonflammable. Paint manufacturers claim it is as washable as a flat alkyd paint, but this isn't quite true. The surface is slightly chalky; it absorbs smudges and tends to wear under vigorous scrubbing, especially if it gets dirty enough to require abrasive cleansers. If you need a scrubbable surface instead, you'll be happier using one of the alkyd paints mentioned below. The flat finish will show dirt more readily than a semi-gloss, but will reduce glare making it suitable for most walls and ceilings.

Semi-gloss and full gloss latex paints have the same properties as flat latex: easy application, quick drying, little odor. In addition they are more resistant to grease and dirt, and easy to

The miracle of latex paints is how easy they are to clean. The kitchen sink and plain water has replaced the mess and smell of cans of turpentine.

If you plan to use both latex and alkyd paints in the same room but want them both the same color, don't worry. Most colors are available in both water and oil base, and in any finish.

clean with detergent rather than abrasive cleansers. Over a primer coat, semi- and full gloss latex can be used on new masonry, dry walls, plaster, wallboard, kitchen and bathroom walls, wood trim, wood and aluminum windows and even baseboard heat ducts.

With some latex paints one coat on top of a primer coat will be sufficient. Of course if you're covering an extremely porous material or a much darker color you may need two or more as full and semi-gloss paints are in general less opaque than flat ones. If you are repainting full or semi-gloss latex over an already glossy surface, you may find out another disadvantage of latex paint. When dry, the gloss finishes are slightly elastic and don't adhere well to a slick surface. The result is peeling. If faced with this situation roughen the surface, with some very fine sandpaper, prime with flat paint first, or use an alkyd paint instead of latex.

Oil Base Paints

Alkyds are a fairly recent addition to the dealer's line of easy-to-handle paints. Made with resins, they are "dripless" because of their jelly-like consistancy in the can. They spread smoothly and quickly. They are thinned with turpentine or a paint thinner. They dry in 3 to 4 hours and, though not as odor-free as latex paints, they are nowhere near as overpowering as the old-fashioned oil-base paints. Clean-up requires mineral solvents rather than water, and is of course rather a nuisance. If you have older alkyd paints around the house, they may contain toxic lead. New alkyd paints do not.

Flat alkyds are more washable and scuff resistant than flat latex paints. Over a primer, they are suitable for use on dry walls, new masonry plaster, wallboard, wood paneling, wood trim, stair risers, aluminum and wood windows, metal cabinets, radiators, pipes and heat ducts.

Semi-gloss and high gloss alkyd enamels retain their luster through much scrubbing and use, and for this reason are better choices for high-traffic areas such as kitchens, bathrooms and hallways, and for tables, chairs, bookshelves, doors and window sills. With proper priming, they too can be used on any of the surfaces listed under flat alkyds.

These days paint manufacturers sell "one-coat" paints. They are extremely thick, like the one at the top above, which is about the consistency of sour cream. If you were to thin the paint to a normal consistency however, like the paint at the bottom, you would get poor coverage. These thick paints are surprisingly easy to apply.

Paint For Special Purposes

Epoxy enamels are extremely tough. They have a hard glossy film that resists dirt, solvents, grease, water and abrasion. They'll hold up under frequent cleaning and are recommended for hallways, playrooms, workshops, launderies, kitchens, and bathrooms. Some epoxy paints come mixed in one container. Others come in two cans which must be mixed together prior to application. Epoxy paints are more expensive but if you need a strong surface, the extra money will be well spent.

Deck and floor enamels come in three types: latex, alkyd and polyurethane. The latter is the most durable, although all will provide hard scuff-resistant surfaces. Check instructions before applying deck enamels to see if a special primer is needed for the surface you are painting.

Aluminum paints, which are resistant to water and therefore inhibit rust, are necessary first coats for heat ducts, radiators, pipes, aluminum and steel window frames and other raw metal surfaces. They also can be used as a sealer for wood surfaces and old masonry. They are best applied by spraying. If you use a brush, stroke in one direction.

Do you have a problem surface? Chances are there's a paint to cover it. If you need to paint a Franklin stove, you can buy a heat-resistant paint. If your surface is particularly moist, you can buy one that's mildew resistant. There are paints that will cover metals, rubber, plastic, cement and fiberglass.

If you're not sure which paint you want, buy from a paint dealer or home decorating center rather than "off the shelf" in a department store. Many smaller stores, because they don't carry a full line of paints, will tell you that what you're looking for doesn't exist. Find a large dealer. The expertise of someone who knows paints can save you time and money.

Other rust-inhibiting paints such as Rustoleum or Derusto work because of the chemicals in the primer. Thus the primer coat is essential. The top coats in these brand names are simply alkyd enamels.

Lacquers are used to paint small surfaces, usually furniture. You must purchase lacquer thinner as a solvent to clean brushes. Lacquers dry in less than an hour (and for this reason are difficult to apply) and give a hard finish. They are available in both high sheen and dull. To deal with the quick drying time, apply two very thin coats, or buy as a spray.

Clear Finishes And Stains

Shellac is used as a sealer for new wood or to give clear protection to wood trim, furniture, floor and stairs. Sand lightly between coats of shellac. Apply paste wax as a final coat to bring out lustre and protect from water stains. The only solvent for shellac is alcohol.

Varnishes can be used on trim and wood paneling. Though it forms a coat which resists moisture and dirt, the glossy varnishes do scratch easily. A coat of paste wax can help prevent scratching. Varnishes come in flat, semi-gloss, satin and glossy finishes.

Stains which provide a "natural" wood finish in a variety of woody colors are easy to apply. Oil stains are the best for do-it-yourself jobs. There are very few water stains left on the market, and application of varnish stains is better left to the professional because of the difficulty in applying them. They dry very quickly; it takes experience not to leave brush marks and to achieve a "wood grain" finish. Oil stains can simply be brushed on and wiped down with a rag. Use on thoroughly sanded trim, wood paneling, furniture, even stairs and floors. Sand lightly between coats. When good and dry, a well rubbed in coat of paste wax can provide protection against scratches.

Many people wonder whether it is worth the trouble to store leftover paint. Here's the consensus of the experts: Little dabs aren't worth saving unless you'll be using them within a month or so. A large quantity can be stored for several months if tightly sealed. When re-opening, skim off the "skin" — don't stir it into the paint.

Some people avoid the skin formation by carefully pouring a thin layer of solvent onto the surface of the paint before storage. Use water for latex paints, linseed oil for oil-base paints, and recap firmly. When you next use the paint, spoon off as much of the protective layer as you can instead of stirring it into the paint.

Store any paint in a cool area, but remember that freezing will ruin it entirely.

6-inch masonry brush

round sash brush

4-inch wall brush

2-inch trim brush

1-inch trim brush

beveled trim brush

An ideal brush inventory for the perfectionist painter will include all of the above. The 4-inch brush is used on most large areas. The 6-inch brush, though heavy to use, is excellent for priming and painting porous masonry surfaces. A variety of trim brushes comes in handy if your woodwork is at all fancy. For very simple jobs the 1-inch trim brush is essential. The small touch-up brush can be a life saver if trim painting isn't your forte.

Painting Equipment

Brushes

There are two schools of thought on brushes for the amateur painter: one says that good quality counts and a good set of lasting brushes is worth the expense. The other says that it's just as good to buy cheap ones, use them until they are worn (hopefully not until the end of the job) and then toss them out. Whichever you choose to do will depend on the scope of the job, whether or not you're likely to use them again in the near future, the time you want to spend cleaning them, and the room you have to store them.

It's true that good brushes hold more paint than cheap ones. This is because their bristles are "flagged" or split on the ends. Hog bristles have natural flags, but the brush doesn't wear well for latex paints because washing softens the bristles too much. Nylon bristles, which wash well have largely replaced hog bristles; they are synthetically flagged. Quality bristles will feel springy and elastic and won't fan excessively if pressed on a flat surface. Check for loose bristles by fanning them. If any bristles at all come loose, many more will come loose as you paint, spelling trouble later on. If you're going for quality, also check to see that the ferrule (the band around the brush) is either aluminum or stainless steel.

The surface to be covered and the kind of paint used will influence your choice of brush. Best for applying latex paints are what is called calcimine brushes which have long sturdy bristles. The flatter, chisel-shaped brushes are right for alkyd paints, varnishes and lacquers since their shape helps spread paint smoothly without leaving lap marks. Very rough surfaces such as cement or stucco require a wide brush with stiff durable bristles.

Two brushes, one for walls and one for trim will get you through most short jobs. If you plan to do a whole interior, you may want to invest in trim brushes in two or three sizes, and a sash brush. These come in angled, flat or square shapes; each is designed for efficiency on various trim shapes.

Choice of handle style is up to you. Remember that you'll be holding it for an extended period of time — take care to buy one that fits your hand.

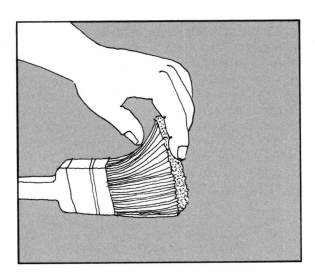

Good brushes have "flagged" tips which resemble hairs with split ends. The "flags" help hold the paint once the brush has been dipped. Spread bristles as shown to check to see that the bristles are set solidly. If you notice loose bristles, don't buy it.

Take a look at the interior of a brush before you buy. Brushes with sparse bristles may have a large gap at the heel which can be a hiding place for paint. As paint builds up it will produce runs and drips when you least expect it. Paint build-up also makes the brush heavier and harder to clean.

Rollers

With rollers as with brushes, there is divided opinion about whether quality equipment is worth the money. Again, what you buy depends on the size of the job. If it's one wall, and you are not likely to paint again for some time, there is little sense in spending a lot of money when a two dollar roller — tray included — will do.

If you have a lot of painting to do, and you opt for quality, here's what to look for in a roller. Make sure the handle allows the cover to slip on and off the core easily for cleaning, yet does not slip while in use. Make sure that the core is of open construction, like a cage rather than a solid tube, since that will avoid the cover "freezing" to it as it dries after cleaning. Make sure that the cover is formed over plastic or something similar which will not soften with repeated use.

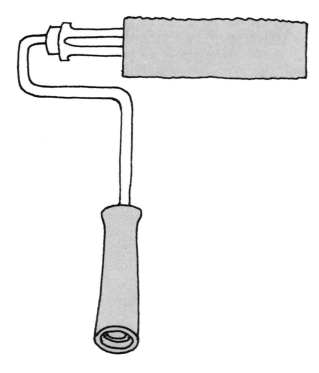

The cover nap is determined by the surface to be painted. Use rollers with ¼-inch nap for most jobs which require a smooth finish. A ⅜ or ¾-inch nap is needed for rough surfaces such as cement or stucco.

Covers are made from synthetic materials, mohair and even lamb's wool. Synthetics will work with most types of paint. Lamb's wool has a tendency to mat if used with enamels. You'll need one 7 or 9-inch roller for large wall areas. If you plan to paint your ceiling with a roller, check that the handle end is hollow and threaded to receive an extension pole. Either a special pole sold in paint stores can be screwed into the handle, or any ordinary screw-type wooden broom pole. You can buy short rollers for trim, and cone-shaped and v-shaped rollers for corners, though all that extra washing up may not be worth it. Some stores sell jumbo rollers which can make your work go faster, provided you can manage them. They are very heavy to use.

Daubers

Other non-brush paint applicators are the daubers, which range from a short flat rectangular pile pad with a handle, to lamb's wool mittens for smearing paint by hand. Unlikely as it may seem, daubers can be efficient painting tools because with each application you bring more paint to the surface than you can with a brush.

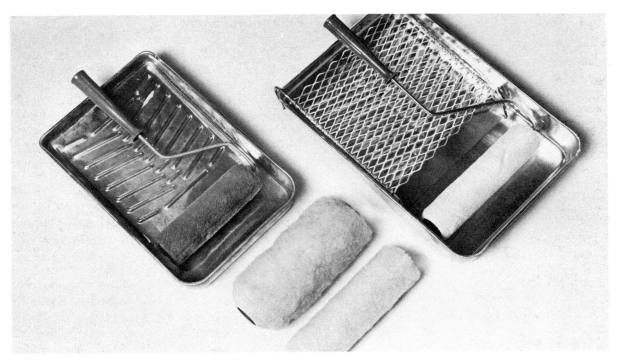

The most recent applicator is the foamed urethane brush pad. Some have reusable handles, others are cheap enough to discard after use. Though they won't take the abuse a good brush can take, they are excellent for close work around trim and windows because the pointed foam tip does not become wider as you apply pressure to the surface.

Buckets And Pans

Even if you'll only be working from one can of paint you'll find it handy to have a bucket in which to pour small quantities to carry about the room or on a ladder. A cheap metal or sturdy paper bucket is fine but even more helpful are the small-size plastic household buckets that have bail handles. If you are working from quart cans, you'll want to transfer the paint into a bucket to make brush dipping easier and keep your hands cleaner.

Painting with rollers requires a roller pan that fits the width of your roller. Extra width won't hurt since it will provide a larger area for rolling on paint. Some pans have attachments for bracing to ladder platforms; others have stabilizing "feet". Neither are really necessary. But you can save time by using a deep roller pan which will hold more paint and cut down on the number of times you have to fill it.

Daubers and pads can simplify covering hard-to-reach nooks and crannies in woodwork and trim.

Rollers with a ¼-inch nap are used for most surfaces. Buy a longer nap for stucco, brick or concrete. A trim roller is handy for small areas.

Cone and V-shaped rollers are also available. They are designed for corners but take a bit of experience to manage efficiently. You may want to do corners with a brush instead.

The new urethane foam brushes which come in several widths are great for trim. They are hard to clean, but cheap enough to toss after use.

You may find the metal grate shown in the roller pan above helpful in rolling excess paint off your roller.

Other Equipment

A strong step ladder with a stable platform to place the paint bucket or pan is a help for painting ceilings, but lots of people get along fine on an old kitchen chair. You may even want to devise a larger platform by using a step ladder connected to a step stool, sawhorse or another ladder by a sturdy plank. This saves getting down to move the ladder and paint after finishing each section, but it's only worth the trouble if it's a pretty big ceiling.

An extension handle for rollers is extremely useful for ceilings and a big help on walls if you don't like to work on ladders. Buy or rent one from your paint store unless you can produce a screw-type broom handle at home that is guaranteed not to wobble.

Newspapers, rags and drop cloths are required "equipment" in any amateur paint job. If you don't own any, old sheets or curtains can serve as substitutes, or you can buy inexpensive crepe-paperish dropcloths from a home decorating center. The thin plastic drop cloths they might try to sell you will drive you crazy, as a drop of paint on them sticks to your shoes and your shoes then drag the whole cloth around. They're all right though for draping over furniture. Sponges and a clean bucket of water are an asset when working with latex since spills and spatters can be wiped away immediately. Rags

with a bottle of turpentine form the core of your emergency kit when working with non-water-base paints. For the least frustration, plan to wear old clothes that can be tossed out or saved for other work days when you're through.

Masking tape is good for protecting surfaces such as window panes. Thin cardboard sheets (you can make them from cereal boxes or use those that back shirts that have been laundered) are useful as shields to protect surfaces such as floors while painting baseboards, and to achieve a straight edge where painting trim.

If your room has no door, or it's impractical to close it because you'll lack ventilation, use a folding gate (or makeshift barricade) to keep pets and young children from the room as you work.

Other tools which will come in handy while painting are a screwdriver for prying off can lids, a hammer for replacing them (by tapping gently around the edge), a nail for punching a few holes in the groove of the can rim to drain out paint that accumulates there when pouring. Stirring sticks usually come free with paints, but better check to be sure they've been included in the package with your paints.

If you are working with latex paints, you might want to borrow a soup ladle from the kitchen to avoid pouring paint into buckets or trays. It will wash up easily with water.

If you are using a roller, have a pair of scissors handy to snip off nap that might fringe at the ends as the fringe can leave lap marks.

Keep a roll of aluminum foil handy too, for wrapping brushes and rollers and covering trays and buckets to prevent them from drying out when you are not working.

You will need spackle, wood putty or joint compound for patching small cracks and dents, and either a putty knife or a small kitchen spatula for smoothing the material. A piece of fine sandpaper is good for the final smoothing.

There are other special tools you might need to cope with problems — sanders, scrapers and so on. To be sure you have everything you need, read through the sections on preparing the room, cleaning up and special problems. When you've accumulated all you need, gather your painting equipment in one spot in the room to be painted, to avoid searching the house later with paint-splotched hands and clothes.

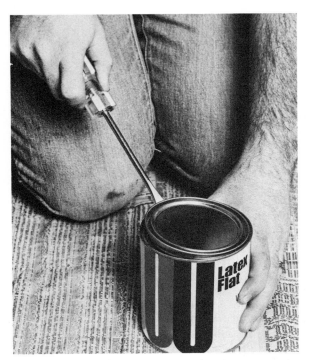

Open paint cans by gently prying up around the rim with a screwdriver. Take care not to bend the rim out of shape.

Close a paint can by lightly tapping the lid back on with a hammer. Tap first in one place, then directly opposite, and continue until lid is secure. If you're going to store the paint for any length of time, cover with a sheet of plastic wrap before replacing lid.

Estimating Time

You may want to have some estimate of the time it'll take you to complete the job. At left is a chart geared to the mythical "average" amateur. Use it only as a rough guide since it doesn't encompass goofs, spills, phone interruptions or time to get "into the swing" of painting. Your paint job will be a success if you don't rush. Plan coffee breaks every two or three hours. Not only will they help you catch your breath, they will also give you time to step back and take a look at the good job you're doing! Plan on being exhausted in seven hours, and completing the job if necessary the following day.

Preparing The Room

Discouraging as it may be, some preparation of the room and wall surfaces is essential to a successful and tension-free paint job. On these pages are tips for preparing a new room or previously-painted room in good shape. Rooms with special preparation problems (filling holes, painting new wood or plaster, damp spots, mold) will be discussed in a few pages.

Clearing The Room

First, remove small furniture pieces like lamps, clocks and so on from the room entirely. Group large pieces in the center of the room so you can get to the walls, and cover with drop cloths. Remove curtains and blinds, and the rods or fixtures that hold them. Remove switch and wall plug plates, mirrors, pictures, and those picture hangers in places that you may want to change. Most people don't bother pulling out picture hooks that will be used again, but the perfectionist would take out everything.

If absolutely necessary, remove doors. Don't unscrew the hinges — just drive up the pin on each hinge and pull it out. If the door isn't too heavy, one person can lift it off the hinges. But if you feel you can get at doors to paint them in place, by all means leave them up and only remove handles or knobs to avoid painting around them.

Painting Tasks	Square Feet Per Hour
finishing smooth plaster walls	
primer and sealer	100
flat-finish paints	90
gloss or semi-gloss finish paints	100

Note: Allow 20% less time for each additional coat. Allow up to 30% more time if your walls are extremely porous, as rough plasters are, and stucco, and so on.

finishing interior wood trim	
puttying and sanding	100
priming and sealing	150
painting (first coat)	70
painting (each additional coat)	80
enameling	40
shellacking and varnishing	100
staining	100

Note: Time should be allowed if sanding and puttying are required between coats, as for varnishing.

finishing ceilings	
primer and sealer	80
flat-finish paint	70
gloss or semi-gloss paints	60

Note: Each additional coat will take about 20% less time.

painting floors	
first coat	150
additional coats	160

painting brick or cement blocks	
first coat	60
additional coats	80

Patching Cracks And Dents

Next, with a can of spackle, patching plaster, wood putty or joint compound, fill small dents and cracks. Simply press the material into the crack or dent and level with a putty knife or a kitchen spatula. Wipe to a smooth surface. Let dry an hour or so before painting so that it won't leave a dull spot under your coat of paint, and sand it flat if you didn't get it smooth enough. Again, for the perfectionist a coat of shellac will make sure the spot isn't porous. Joint compound should dry overnight before painting.

Cleaning And Sanding

Wipe areas over windows and doors where dust might have accumulated. Wipe surfaces with light dirt build-up with a damp cloth or sponge. It may be a good idea to dust your walls if they are sooty or dirty too. Some experts say to give them a light sanding, but that sounds like a lot of work. Woodwork that has been previously painted with high or semi-gloss paint may be a problem. To rough up the surface a bit for better adhesion, you can sand them. Or you could use an oil-base paint instead of latex. Or you could ignore advice and hope for the best. Remember to wipe all room surfaces after any sanding to remove the dust which could ruin your finish. In kitchens and bathrooms where the walls may have a film of dirt or grease, scrub them vigorously, using a strong household cleanser.

Check radiators, pipes and baseboard heat ducts for rust spots, and remove rust with a wire brush or, in severe cases, with rust remover. New metals should be cleaned of their protective grease and any rust spots. A good washing with detergent will get rid of grease.

When everything is clean and dust-free, protect your floor area with drop cloths arranged flat so you don't trip over rumples. Newspapers can be used in light traffic areas, but they tend to rip or bunch up if you walk on them a lot. Keep extra newspapers at hand, however; they'll be helpful to shove up against baseboards when you paint them.

The plates on switches and plugs screw off the wall. If you are worried about children around open wiring, disconnect fuses first, or if you live in an apartment, ask the handyman to help you. If the plates are to be painted, do it separately and let them dry well before you screw them back.

A flexible kitchen spatula is a perfectly good tool for patching small cracks, dents or holes.
When the hole is filled, smooth it as best you can with the spatula.
If the surface is raised or rough when the filling compound has dried, sand it smooth with a fine sandpaper.

Priming

It is unlikely that you have new plaster walls these days, but if you do and they haven't had time to "cure", you should wait two to three months before painting. If this is impossible, prime the walls with one coat of latex primer or paint. The water base will allow the excess moisture to escape while the plaster continues to dry. If you want the final finish to be oil-base, coats of oil-base paint can be applied over the primer after the curing period.

New wallboard must also be primed with a coat of latex primer or paint, as oil-base paints may leave a rough surface as a primer coat. Either latex or oil-base can be used as subsequent coats.

Unpainted woodwork needs to be sealed too. Use an enamel undercoat for woods to be painted with either oil-base or latex paint. A latex paint might leave a rough surface if used as an undercoat on raw wood.

New metal surfaces need to be coated with a primer selected according to what kind of metal you're working with (see page 42), and metal surfaces that tend to rust should be primed with a rust-resistant primer. Never paint any heating fixtures while they are hot because they'll peel. Wait until pipes are cool.

Painting The Ceiling

Ceilings should always be painted first for the obvious reason that spatters on the walls and trim can be covered later. Ceilings are usually painted white or a lighter tone of the wall color so they will reflect as much light as possible into the room. Before you start, decide whether or not you'll paint the molding too. Usually if the walls are to be painted, the ceiling molding is painted the same color as the walls. If the walls are to be papered, the molding is painted the same color as the ceiling.

If possible, paint facing a window or have a light focused on your work area to determine how well you are covering. With latex paints you can go back and touch up thin spots, but retouching isn't as successful with alkyds.

Protect your floor and furniture. Even the most painstaking home painters leave drops and splatters. You'll have a better time if you don't have to worry about making a mess.

If you are going to use a roller, it won't reach quite into the upper corners. Begin by using a brush to paint around the perimeter of the ceiling, or do this as you roll. Plan to do the roller work across the width of the ceiling. Begin in a corner by brushing a 2-foot strip along the wall. With the roller, work back and forth into the brushed strip. Use criss-cross strokes to assure complete coverage.

After replenishing the roller, begin in a dry area and work toward the one you just painted. You can minimize splattering by never allowing the roller to spin, but no matter how careful you are you'll soon find out why painters wear hats. If you wear glasses, you might want to check and clean them often, rather than wait until paint has dried on them and has to be scraped off.

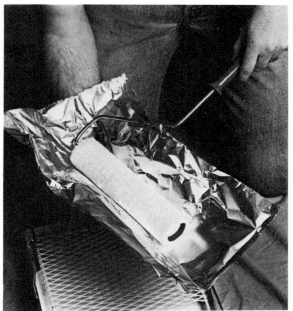

Schedule a couple of breaks for yourself if you're painting a ceiling alone. Wrap your roller and cover your pan with foil if you plan to stop for more than a few minutes.

Set up a stepladder platform (two stepladders with a strong plank between) if you're using a brush to paint the ceiling. We certainly don't recommend using a brush, but if you do, plan to work along the width, not the length of the ceiling, in strips about 2 feet wide so you can begin the second strip before the first has dried, reducing the possibility of lap marks.

If you really want to paint your ceiling with a brush, prevent drips and splattering by not dipping more than a third of the bristles into the paint. Always work from a wet edge into the unpainted area after redipping your brush.

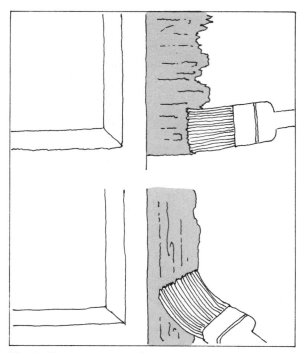

"Cutting" close to woodwork means holding the brush at right angles to the corner, placing the tip in the corner made by the wall and the woodwork, and stroking away from corner. A parallel stroke is then used to smooth the work while it is still wet.

A brush dipped further than a third its bristle length into paint will only drip and mess up the job. If that much paint doesn't seem to go far enough, it is probably because your brush is too small or too poor in quality.

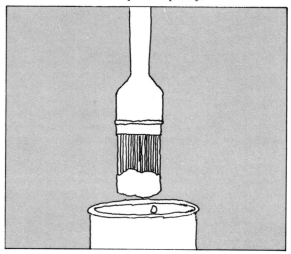

Painting The Walls

You'll most likely choose to paint most walls with a roller. Nevertheless, brushwork comes in handy in corners to "outline" around door and window frames, and where surfaces are too small to bother with a roller as in some tiny kitchens and crowded bathrooms. There are some tricks to using a brush well.

Working With Brush And Roller

Dipping a brush correctly is an art. Slowly immerse it into the pan, covering only one third of the length of the bristles. Gently slap the brush against one side of the bucket to remove excess paint. Do not apply to a wall without removing the excess or you will have to cope with dripping problems. Submerging the brush to the ferrule wastes time and paint as it leads to paint buildup in the base of the brush which causes the paint to run and shortens the brush life. It will drip all over your hands anyway.

Remove stray bristles on the brush as they appear with shears or a wall scraper to avoid awkward streaks. Watch for bristles that get left on the wall. Pick them up with the tip of your brush — they'll stick to it — not your fingers, to avoid large wall marks. Cover marks left by the brush tip with gradual smoothing strokes.

"Outline" close work around ceilings, doors and windows with a brush before you use the roller. With paints which don't show lap marks easily (and these are most likely the paints you have) you can do this throughout the room, and then switch to a roller. With paints that do produce lap marks outline with a brush as you roll. Naturally; two people can do this better than one.

"Cut" close to the woodwork with your brush (using a cardboard shield if necessary) by placing the tip of the brush in the corner. Paint a few inches outwards from the corner for several strokes, stroke parallel to the woodwork once or twice to smooth the area, and end the stroke by lifting the brush toward the wall and away from the trim. Never paint with the side of your brush or the bristles will mat and the paint will splatter. When you have finished outlining the area you want, load your roller by rolling it in the deeper end of the roller tray and removing the excess on the slanted part. Load as much paint as possible without dripping it on the floor. Start in a corner or near, but not next to, a door or window you've outlined. Use up part of the paint on a flat surface then roll as close to the trim as possible to cover the brush texture with that of the roller. Take care not to smear the trim.

On large surfaces follow the same criss-cross, every-which-way stroke suggested for ceilings. Following a uniform back and forth or up and down pattern can cause streaking.

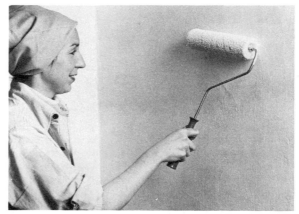

Whether applying a first or second coat with a roller, always roll in an irregular criss-cross method, never in a regular up-and-down or back-and-forth pattern.

Roll close to a corner or to the trim, carefully covering the existing brush marks to the extent possible. The job will turn out better if two people do it; one does the brushing, the other follows with a roller while the brush work is still wet. You can tell whether a second coat will be needed as soon as any portion of the first coat is dry. Since latex paints dry very fast, you can save yourself time by checking the first bit of wall as soon as it is dry. If it looks streaky or spotty, you know you will need a second coat, and can do a quicker, less perfect job on the first coat throughout the rest of the room.

Painting Trim

For most trim, if the area is going to get moderate to heavy use, you'll be switching to a paint that gives a full or semi-gloss, or satin finish, since flat wall paint won't wash or wear well. You can, however, use flat wall paint on moldings and window areas where washability isn't important; that's the only way to get a perfect color match if you want it. Your wall paint can be color matched with satin, and full and semi-gloss enamels, but the texture and sheen will make the color look slightly darker. Use glossy enamel on trim in bathrooms, kitchens and in windows that frost or fog for better water resistance.

Make whatever sanding, hole-filling and cleaning preparations are necessary. If trim is in bad shape, see our special problems section. Remove whatever knobs, handles, cranks and hinges you can from windows, cabinets and doors. Place your trim brushes, along with your wall brush on a roller pan or a piece of aluminum foil for easy selection. Most paints need stirring, even if they have been shaken by the dealer's machine. The label will tell you if you are not supposed to stir the one you're using. Transfer a small quantity of paint into an easy-to-hold container and you're ready to begin.

It's logical to note here some general hints for brushing trim: use the same dip-and-tap method for loading brushes described in the section on walls. Hold the brush near the base of the handle for better close-work control. Don't apply so much pressure that the bristles fan, but press hard enough to make them flex a bit at the tip as you begin each stroke. Brush slowly on wood so that bristles have time to force paint into each tiny grain depression in the surface. Slow brushing will cover better and save you time in the long run. If a back-and-forth stroke is too hard to control, paint towards the wet edge to feather the brush marks into one another.

If brushing proves to be too frustrating for you on complicated trim areas, try a dauber or a urethane foam brush. You may find the going a bit easier.

Baseboard is sometimes the first trim to be done by professionals, but you may want to save it until last to avoid scuffing or stirring up dust that would settle on it and ruin its finish. Windows are done before doors, and doors before such things as built-in shelves and cupboards. Let's look specifically at tips for painting each of them.

Windows

Some people like to protect glass areas; others like to paint without a tape or shield, figuring that it's easier to remove paint with a razor blade when it's dry. This method has the recommended advantage that the extra paint acts as a sealer between the wood and glass. Taping is done with masking tape (same thing as freezer tape). Remove it from the glass as soon as the paint dries, because hot sun can bake the tape on so it's very hard to remove. If you want some protection but hate to tape, cut newspaper the size of the window, wet the window and apply the paper, which will hold until you've finished. Don't worry about a little overlap on the glass — it's good protection.

There are two secrets to trouble-free window painting: one, paint from the center out toward the sides and two, paint horizontal pieces with sideways strokes, vertical pieces with up and down strokes.

For example, on a casement window, first paint the muntins (the strips between the panes), next the casing, then the frame, and finally the sill and the apron below it.

If you have double hung windows which can be opened, pull down the upper sash and raise the lower to get at the "meeting rail." Paint the bottom, front and top of the meeting rail, then proceed to the muntins for as far as you can paint. Paint the bottom of the lower sash and then the top of the upper sash. Next paint the tracks in which the upper sash slides. Close the lower sash leaving a tiny space between the sash and sill. Paint the muntins of the top sash, then continue with the rest of the sash. Paint the tracks in which the lower sash slides, then move to the casings. Paint the top of the frame, moving to one side then the other. Once paint is dry, open and close the window several times to unstick the sashes. Don't close completely unless you are absolutely sure paint is dry or windows may stick permanently. If windows don't open as easily as before try gently rubbing the dry tracks with waxpaper or using a special commercial silicone solution sold in hardware stores.

Window painting is the most time-consuming of all trim jobs. Don't let it become the most frustrating. Try several brushes, including a round sash brush, until you find one that seems to speed your work. Smears on glass are very easy to scrape off later.

On muntins, casing and frame, brush horizontal pieces with a horizontal stroke, vertical pieces with a vertical stroke. Brush back and forth (or up and down) wherever you can. Where you can't, stroke in one direction only, but towards the area you just painted to feather the brush marks.

After paint has dried and you've opened and closed the window a few times, it's still good to leave it open a crack for a day or so, to make sure there's no chance it will seal itself shut.

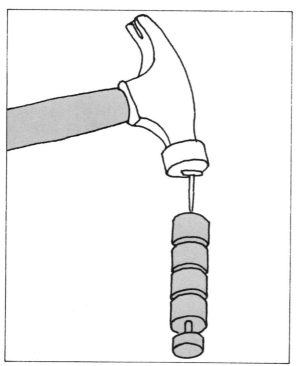

To take down a door, remove the hinge pin from the door by tapping gently from the bottom with a nail or phillips screwdriver and a hammer, and then lifting the pin out from the top. Do not unscrew the hinges unless absolutely necessary.

To replace the door simply line up the hinge sections and drop the hinge pin in from the top. Tap gently with a hammer if it doesn't fall into place easily. If the door is heavy, this is a two-person job.

Watch for paint build-up in corners of paneled doors. Remove it with a "pulling out" stroke which begins as shown and ends in the air after you have drawn the extra paint out of the corner. A flip of the wrist once you've removed the brush from the surface helps prevent excess from dripping.

If you are doing one side then another, therefore turning the door just as one coat dries, make soft braces out of rags or sponges for the just-dried coat to rest on. Hard materials may cause marks.

Doors

You can paint flush doors with a roller or a brush. In either case, its probably easier to take the door off (pull hinge pins — do not take off hinges) and lay it flat. Working on a flat surface allows you to give the door a good thick application without risk of runs or sags in the finish. Apply one coat to one side, allow it to dry, then turn it over and do the other. Go back to the original first side when dryness permits turning.

Panelled doors are probably best removed too. Do them the way you'd do windows: from the center out, stroking back and forth or up and down to match the section. When the central parts are done, paint the inside panels of the casing, then outside of the casing. Remember to "feather" (a light, curved stroke) where vertical and horizontal strokes meet to blend them. If you experience paint build-up in the corners of the panels use a "pull out" stroke which simply means slowly working the bristles into the corner, twisting the hand a bit then lifting the brush, letting the bristles absorb the excess paint. Try to end the stroke in the air to avoid bristle marks.

If the door swings into a room of a different color, the latch edge is usually painted to match the room it swings into. On the hinge edge, use the color of the room the door swings out of.

If you want to paint a paneled door in two colors (panels one color, crossmembers and stiles another) you will really have to remove the door and lay it flat since this will make cutting close to the many edges much easier. Don't tape areas to protect them unless you're willing to wait hours until the paint is completely dry. Otherwise the tape will remove the edges of your new coat. Use a cardboard shield if you don't have confidence in your cutting stroke.

If you want to disguise some door hardware by painting it along with the door, pay particular attention that drips and runs don't result. If the hardware is likely to get knocked or chipped, sand and prime it for extra paint adhesion. Don't paint knobs unless you're working with a very tough glossy enamel.

Shelves

Shelves are an exercise in painting in confined spaces. Realizing that before you begin will save you from becoming impatient during the job. If you can't find a brush with a short enough handle to facilitate painting tops and bottoms of unremoveable shelves, cut one to fit your needs.

Satin finishes are good for shelves since they take the wear and tear of books being slid in and out yet they won't give you the glare produced by such a large surface covered with full or semi-gloss.

If you've just built the shelves you'll need to prepare them for painting: fill nail holes, sand and seal the wood with a primer. The one you select will depend on the paint that is to be applied after.

If the shelves aren't new, wash or dust them well, sanding if necessary.

If they have shelf tracks in them, remove the shelf braces — paint them separately if you want them to blend in. The tracks will cause dripping if you paint them with a freshly-dipped brush. Cover them with a "dry" brush — it'll take more strokes but you won't have paint creeping from behind the tracks a half hour after you've finished the job.

Removable shelves should be taken out and painted separately so as not to miss areas that may one day show should you adjust shelf heights.

Sometimes shelves can be more easily painted with a short roller, outlining first, of course, with a brush. If you have a wall of shelves, try both tools to see which is easier for you.

Baseboards

Baseboards present no special problems. They require a good cutting stroke and in most cases the use of a cardboard shield or sheet of newspaper to protect the floor. When working with shields, change them often to avoid making more of a mess than you would have without. If masking tape won't harm your floor use that as a shield. Start at the top edge of the baseboard, paint a foot or two then paint the bottom edge.

Avoid a lot of traffic in a room in which the baseboard has just been painted, so that dust doesn't settle on it and mar the finish.

If your room is carpeted take special care to cover the floor. In rare cases it may even be easier to remove the baseboard, paint it elsewhere and replace it. However, that's a formidable job and if at all possible spend your extra energy rearranging drop cloths and using a metal shield to protect the carpet.

In baseboard painting, a stiff paper, cardboard or sheet of metal forms is often recommended as a useful barrier between your brush and the floor. Our own experience indicates that newspaper, which can be replaced constantly, works better.

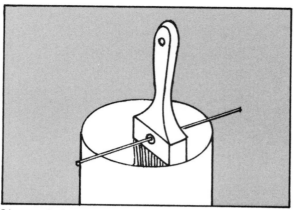

It's a good idea to drill holes in the handles of your brushes before using them so you can string them on a wire in a can of solvent during breaks on the job or overnight. After final cleaning, wipe off excess turpentine with a clean rag or brush gently on a rough but clean surface.

Brushes used with latex can simply be held under a faucet — work the bristles with your fingers to remove all paint that might be build up near the heel.

Cleaning Up

Paint Cans

You may find a crust of thick paint on your paint can that prevents you from sealing it well. This might have been avoided by piercing the indented rim with a nail in several places so paint could drip through, but it's too late now, so clean out the rim with the corner of a piece of cardboard, or scrape it with a screwdriver before sealing the lid on the can.

Brushes

If you've invested in quality brushes you'll want to protect that investment with good cleaning and proper storage.

If you take a break or your work is interrupted for a few hours, wrap your brush in plastic wrap or aluminum foil. Or if there is a hole in your brush handle, you can suspend the brush on a wire in the paint to keep the flagged tips off the bottom. Cover the bucket with foil or plastic wrap and you can leave your brushes for several hours.

If you want to store your brush for a few days until you begin another paint job, hang it in turpentine or linseed oil (or water, if latex is used) and then wipe clean with a cloth or brush on a rough surface when you're ready to begin again.

To clean brushes which have been used to apply oil-base paint for storing for an indefinite period of time, clean in several changes of paint thinner, turpentine or other solvent bought from your dealer. Do this by working the bristles back and forth. Shake or wipe off excess solvent. If necessary, wash with detergent and water until no more paint color can be seen. Comb the bristles with a wide-tooth metal hair comb or a comb bought for this purpose to untangle inner bristles. Let bristles dry, then wrap in foil or stiff paper. Store flat in a dry place.

Brushes that have only been used to apply latex paint are considerably easier to clean. Use warm water and soap if necessary — comb, dry and wrap as described above.

If you are in doubt about the proper way to clean your brushes of other paints or finishes, ask your dealer for advice when you purchase the paint.

Old brushes that have been poorly cleaned

and stored can in most cases be restored to some degree of usability. Soak bristles first in a brush softener and then follow the steps just described.

If you have sensitive skin, wear gloves when using solvents and cleaning preparations.

Daubers and foam applicators are hard to clean. Often they disintegrate before you can get the paint out. If you use them, plan to toss them out after use since trying to clean them takes more time than they are worth.

Rollers And Pans

Good rollers can be stored for short periods of time (even overnight) if you wrap them tightly with foil or plastic. The pan should be covered tightly too.

To clean a roller you want to keep, try to roll out remaining paint on newspapers.

If the roller has been used with latex, run it under a faucet or soak in soapy water. Remove the cover from the handle and manipulate the nap with your fingertips to draw out paint that might be matted underneath. Run under faucet again until water from roller ceases to carry the color of the paint. Squeeze the roller gently, then dry by rubbing it with an absorbent rag or old terrycloth towel. A hair blowdryer works well to complete drying. Clean cage and handle, and slip the roller back on. Store by hanging by handle so as not to cause a flat surface on part of the roller cover.

For rollers used with oil-base paints, use the appropriate solvent instead of water, working not in the sink but in the roller pan or something deeper. Follow the steps described above. Use gloves to protect your skin if you are using a particularly potent solvent. (Turpentine used now and then does not bother most people's skin.)

Roller pans used for latex paint are easy to clean with water if they haven't been used for long. If you've been painting for hours though, there may be a crust on the edges. Scrape it off with a dull knife.

Inexpensive rollers may not be worth the cleaning process since their nap may dry hardened no matter how much attention you give them. For small jobs the "use and toss out" approach is sometimes more efficient if you buy inexpensive rollers and pans.

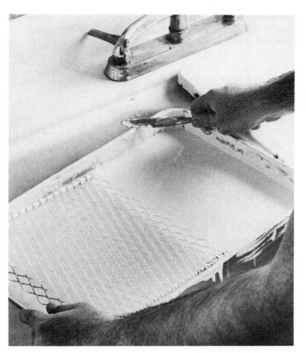

A spatula or kitchen knife can help remove paint hardened on roller pan prior to final cleaning. Other stubborn spots will yield to plastic or copper scouring pads.

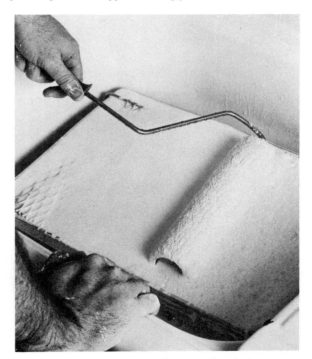

Latex-filled rollers are almost fun to wash – they're so easy. Give them a soap and warm water treatment right in your kitchen sink. Be sure to store them hung up by their handles, not lying flat.

Face, Hands, Hair And Clothes

Naturally, the best way to cut cleanup time is to make as little mess as possible. For most amateurs however, messes are part of painting and trying to be too meticulous can only hamper your confidence. Besides, paint smears on clothes and face are the do-it-yourselfer's trademark — wear them proudly at the end of a project.

Hands are the first things you'll want to clean once you've finished with brushes and pans. If you have painted with oil-base, use turpentine or paint thinner and a clean rag. Work as fast as possible to avoid having to apply several times since the turpentine evaporates quickly. You'll probably have to rub around cuticles. Read the labels before attempting to use any other solvent as some can irritate your skin.

If you have paint on your face or neck, dip a bit of the rag into the turpentine and dab off gently. Be extremely careful near your eyes. Apply oil or lotion to your hands and arms and any other areas cleaned with turpentine to prevent your skin from drying.

Large gobs of paint in your hair are often a problem — again, use turpentine and a rag if there is a substantial amount. Little specks will come out with regular shampooing. (People with long hair should tie it back when painting.) Covering the head with a scarf or one of those paper paint caps is an even better idea. Wear the brim of the cap on the back of your head to avoid leaving its imprint on the wall if you should bend forward while painting.)

If you have oil-base paint on your glasses, don't try to scrape it off as that may scratch them — this is especially true with plastic lenses. Instead, apply a bit of turpentine with a very soft cloth, remove gently and then rinse with soap and water.

If the paint you've been working with is latex, then cleaning will be easy. Soap and water will remove fresh paint with very little effort in most cases. Older paint will flake off by itself in bath or shower. Latex paint on glasses will usually yield to a gentle fingernail.

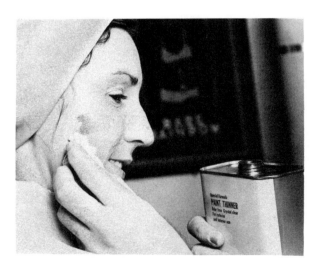

Remove paint from clothes with either turpentine or water, depending on the paint used. Use a scrub brush if necessary. Sometimes dried paint won't come out completely and for this reason it's a good idea to wear old clothes that don't matter. (Everyone should have a set of work clothes that don't fear spots, splashes, oil or dirt.) Don't make the mistake of wearing old clothes that are too large, such as a big workshirt, because they might get in your way or leave marks on the paint while you are moving about or doing close work such as trim.

Remember that turpentine-soaked rags are a fire hazard. Either wash or throw away, putting them in a metal garbage can with a lid right after use.

Floors And Furniture

Smears on floors or furniture should be attended to as soon as possible. Wet paint is easier to remove than dry. Turpentine or solvent is used to remove oil base paint mistakes. If there are only spatters here and there don't wipe a large area with your rag — dab each one individually to prevent smearing. Soapy water and a scrub brush will remove latex. Sometimes dry paint spatters come off a floor easily with a scraper or a dull knife, but be careful if you use one not to gouge the surface.

Windows

Scrape paint from window surfaces with a single-edge razor blade or scraping tool made especially for this purpose. In removing excess paint from glass, remember that it's easier to get off if you catch it after it's only dried a bit. Completely dry paint takes more elbow grease. Many builders suggest leaving an eighth of an inch or so on the glass to act as a sealer between the glass and wood. Suck up scrapings immediately with a vacuum cleaner so they don't stick to nearby paint or become ground into the floor. If the sill isn't completely dry, catch the scrapings with a paper towel to avoid trying to remove them from a sticky surface.

Scrape paint off window glass cautiously if you use a razor blade. Instead of removing excess completely, leave a tiny bit to act as a sealer between the pane and the wood.

Spatter marks can often be removed with a scraper or dull knife if they are completely dry. Be careful not to mar the floor in the process.

When applying plaster to cracks make certain the total area of the crack is filled. Work it in with a putty knife, or your finger if need be.

Scrape off excess plaster, leaving it a bit rough if it's a large hole. Since it may shrink after it has dried, the rough surface will increase the adhesion of your second application.

You need to sand any patch and then seal with a primer before painting.

Preparing Problem Surfaces

Preparation for most painting jobs is routine, but once in a while you will come upon a problem surface that requires special preparation before painting. Most are easily remedied with the proper tools and elbow grease.

Damaged Plaster

Small cracks, holes and dents in plaster can be patched as described on page 21. But when the damaged area is larger, you will have to use a two-step process, and prepare the surface several days in advance. You'll need some type of patching material such as spackle or wall compound, a putty knife, and a brush and primer to coat the damaged area once it has been repaired.

Remove any loose material from the hole or crack with a corner-edge of a razor-blade scraper or putty knife. A screwdriver could be used on the worst cracks and holes.

Be sure to clean soft or breaking plaster at the edges of the hole and also enlarge any part of the opening that may be too small to allow the patching material to enter. Blow out the dust well. With a brush or atomizer, moisten the crack or hole with water — make sure that water penetrates the opening. With a putty knife fill the area completely with your patching compound. Scrape off excess filler and allow to dry completely — at least a day. If the compound has dried without cracks and has not shrunk away from the edges, you can now sand it smooth and prime the area with a coat of shellac. If the plaster has shrunk or cracked, dampen the area again and refill. Let dry, then sand it smooth, and prime.

Very large holes in wallboard take a bit more time, because the wet patching compound won't stick in the hole. Nevertheless you can fix them yourself too with a very professional result. Chip away all loose pieces of plaster. Take a piece of backing support — this can be wire screen mesh or even heavy hardware cloth — and cut it bigger than the hole. Thread a wire through it, put the backing support behind the hole and pull wire through so that it holds the support tightly against the back of the hole. Affix the wire by twisting it to a small piece of wood or a screwdriver or pencil so that it holds the support in place. Mix patching plaster and then, moisten the interior and the perimeter of the hole thoroughly. With a putty knife, apply a coat of plaster around the hole so that it holds the mesh. Let dry. Remove the wood or pencil support and wire. Continue patching and remove excess. Let dry again to check for shrinkage. Once you are satisfied, sand smooth, prime with a sealer and you're ready to paint.

In any patching that requires filling twice due to shrinkage, leave a rough surface after the first coat to allow the second to grip better. In some cases, a third application will be necessary.

If you are patching with plaster on a smooth wall surface you'll probably have no noticable change in texture after you've patched and painted. However, if you are patching a rough surface, you will want to try to match the texture and you can do this easily by adding a bit of sand to your patching material.

If you are patching a surface that has a texture-troweled surface, try to duplicate it as you fill the crack or hole, using the type of trowel that created the original texture if possible. You can sometimes get by just by letting the material harden in rough form. Or you may be able to achieve a match by the stippled effect you get from pressing the patch sponge while the plaster is still wet.

Extra Dirty Surfaces

Scrub vigorously with a solution of water and trisodium phosphate. You can buy it in powered form at most hardware and paint stores. Mix according to package directions, and wear gloves when applying. Rinse well and dry the surface thoroughly so as not to leave any residue on it.

Mildew

Don't try to paint over mildew. Instead, remove from surface with a scrub brush and household bleach. Again, wear gloves to protect your hands.

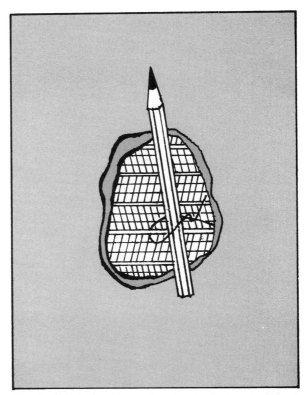

Very large holes in wallboard need a wire backing to support the wet plaster. This illustration shows one method. Another is simply to ball up a long length of soft wire and cram it into the hole before applying patching plaster.

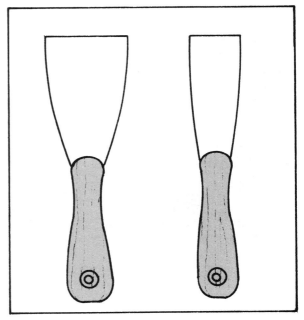

If you've a lot of patching to do, you'll need a good putty knife. Small ones are fine for cracks, but a wide one will work better for a big hole.

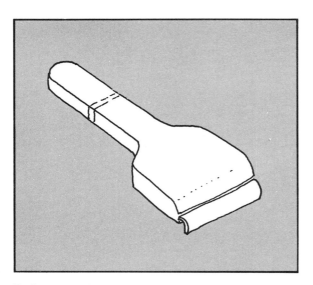

Each time a peeled surface is repainted without preparation, the unevenness shows more. The paint scraper above is the basic tool to get rid of all loose flakes, but a lot of elbow grease is needed to smooth the edges of the peeled portion with sandpaper. The inside of the peel is then carefully primed to raise the level somewhat.

Chipped Or Peeled Paint

In many cases, old paint that has a few chips or gouges is easier to repair bit by bit, than to remove completely. Chips need to be treated because they leave sharp edges which will ruin a smooth paint finish. With a paint scraper knock off loose particles. Then sand by hand with a fine grain sandpaper. With a small brush, "spot-prime" the chipped areas, taking care not to cover surrounding surface that already has paint on it.

Worn Paint

Sometimes you'll need to cover surfaces that have worn spots — such as at the bottom of stairways or near light switches. Sand to remove nicks and to rough up the surface a bit if it has developed a patina. Wipe dust away, prime with a sealer, again taking care not to spread the primer in areas that are already covered.

Glossy Surfaces

If you decide you want to paint a very glossy surface, you may have to prepare it specially. Wood paneling that has been already finished probably only needs washing and sanding a bit if the surface is extremely glossy. If you want to paint a non-wood paneling, most primers adequately prepare the surface. If it is particularly glossy or is constructed from an unusual building material, check with your dealer to make sure that what you've chosen is right.

Pine Paneling

If the paneling is rough you must prime it and take special care to seal over knots and crevices that might give off pitch. Use a shellac sealer for these areas.

Damp Wood

You may run into "wet wood" near windows or doors leading to the outside, or sinks. The paint, no matter how waterproof, won't hold on the wood. You must take steps to dry it if you can't replace it. Sand off what paint remains and then focus a flood light with a 75-watt bulb on the wood to evaporate the moisture. The drying process may take a few days. If the wood starts to actually get hot, your lamp is too close for safety. Keep an eye on it from time to time. Once the wood is dry, prime it with a wood sealer or conditioner specifically recommended to cut down on water penetration. Of course, if the water is coming from behind, you might be able to take steps to protect the wood if you can't actually stop the water intrusion itself.

Gouged Wood

Gouges in wood need special attention. Patch with wood putty or a vinyl patching material, making sure you completely fill the hole. Once the material has set, sand it until smooth, then prime.

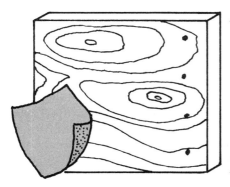 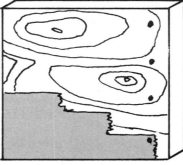 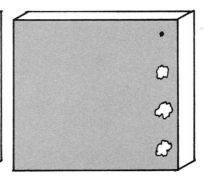

Bare Wood

Never attempt to paint unfinished wood without priming it with a sealer. Make sure the bare surface is clean. (Ground in dirt from construction can be removed with a multisolvent.) Sand lightly, then wipe with a bit of turpentine. When the surface is dry, prime with a sealer that is compatible with the paint you'll be using. (Most labels recommend a primer to be used. If yours doesn't ask the dealer to choose one for bare wood.) Your primer coat is the key to smooth application and good adhesion of the top coats.

Gouges, dents or nail holes in bare wood are usually patched with putty after you prime to prevent chemicals in the filler from injuring the wood. Prime over them quickly before laying on your top coats.

After the primer, bare wood usually requires two coats of paint to give the best finish.

To paint bare or new wood, sand lightly and wipe down with turpentine.

Prime knotholes with shellac, then the entire surface with a primer paint.

Fill nail holes with putty, then apply two coats of the final paint.

Rusted Metal

All rust must go before you apply any paint to metals. You can sometimes remove fine rust with sandpaper. Wire brushes or steel wool will also work. For large rust areas, use a rust remover or an electric wire brush — or a combination of both if the rust is severe. First, take off as much as you can with the rust remover, then after the surface has dried, sand with the wire brush attachment. Coat with a primer that is specifically formulated to prevent rust.

Wallpaper

Only paint over wallpaper if it is indeed paper (not vinyl or foil or fabric), and only if the surface is completely smooth. That means no torn strips, no lapped seams and no areas which look as if they are puffy — that usually means the paper isn't sticking, and it can spell trouble in the future. Make sure the paper is as clean as possible before painting. Pulp papers in general need no priming but it wouldn't hurt to add one if you need to cover a dark color or an obtrusive design. Strip off papers that are strippable. Remove those that aren't by following directions given in the wallpapering section of this book. And of course, unless you really want the textured effect, don't try to paint over flocked materials, even if they are in good shape.

If you are in doubt about preparations for any home painting job, go to a large home decorating center that has consultants on hand to give advice. In most cases the advice is free, and well worth the trip. You can usually find everything you need at one of these stores to solve your preparation problem.

Removing Old Paint

Any time you have to totally remove an old coat of paint, go after it with realistic expectations. It's a tough and time-consuming job, and you'll want to give yourself a good amount of time to do it. If you work on the theory that it won't go fast, and schedule breaks from time to time, you won't get discouraged a quarter of the way through.

There are three ways to remove old paint. You can sand with an electric sander if the coat isn't too thick. This takes conscientious cleaning afterward to remove all the dust from the surface. Either wipe well with a damp cloth or give the surface a sponging with soap and water, rinsing afterward.

You can strip old paint with a paint remover. Jelly types are easier to use than the thin liquids. Work with gloves and try to avoid spattering it on your skin. (If you do get any on your

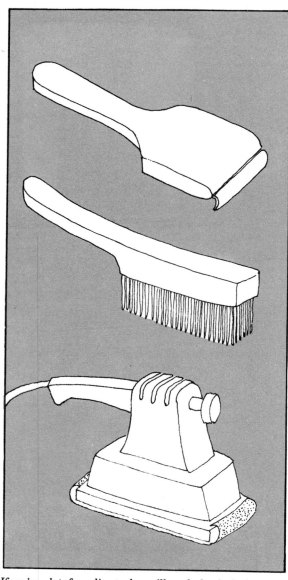

If you've a lot of sanding to do you'll need a hooked-edge wood scraper for peeling paint. A wire brush or steel wool work well for taking off rust. If the sanding job looks like a big one, electric sanders of both the vibrating and belt variety can be rented from paint or hardware stores.

  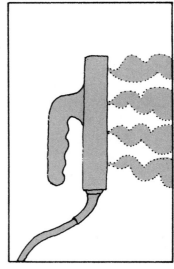

skin, wash copiously under running water.) With a thick brush, apply an ample coat on a small area. Don't try to work on more than three square feet at a time. Using little strokes, work in one direction only. After 15 or 20 minutes (or the time specified on your particular brand of remover) check with a scraper to see how soft the paint is. If you can scrape all the way to the wood, then remove the paint. If not, apply a bit more remover, wait for it to absorb, then try again. In particularly stubborn cases, you may have to scrape what comes off even if you don't reach the wood the first time, reapply, let soften and then apply again. Paint removers create a sludgy residue which must be wiped off with a cloth or steel wool. Once the surface is completely dry (at least five to six hours), sand if necessary. If you think you need to seal the wood, give it a coat of primer. Otherwise, merely wipe it down with turpentine on a rag before painting.

Removing paint with heat is a tricky process and should be done with utmost caution. It is only efficient for large surfaces. If you use a propane torch apply flame quickly to the surface and immediately scrape off paint which will start to "boil" or blister. Leaving it too long will burn the wood. It's likely that it will become a bit scorched — this won't hurt — but do not char it. More sensible equipment for the do-it-yourself painter who wants to use heat is an electric paint softener which can be rented in many paint stores. It uses no flame. You merely press it against the surface, hold a few seconds and then scrape. Some even have built-in scrapers that remove the paint as you move the softener from place to place. In most cases, you'll need to sand the wood after using heat removal methods.

There are three methods for removing paint. Stripping with paint remover is feasible if the surface isn't too large. For large surfaces, the job is unmanageable and too expensive.

Electric sanders, especially belt sanders, do an efficient job — again on smallish areas. The clean-up must be very thorough.

The last resort for a large area is heat removal. Propane torches do the job but must be handled carefully. A better tool is a rented electric paint softener.

Painting Masonry

Before you paint any kind of masonry — bricks, concrete blocks, or concrete walls or floor — you should know something about its nature. New masonry theoretically shouldn't be painted for four to six months since it needs time to harden completely. Also, because there is much alkali in new concrete you must use paints especially made for concrete or you risk having the alkali cause peeling, flaking and chalking (white stains or streaks). Let's look at the kinds of paints that are appropriate.

Paints To Choose

Latex: Latex is the easiest to apply and clean up. Some are especially marketed for concrete, others can be used if label directions specify. Latex generally offers the best color selection and is the most fade-resistant.

Portland Cement: If your concrete surface hasn't ever been painted before, you may use portland cement paint. It comes in a powder and you mix it with water. It provides a very tough and durable coat and you can cover a lot of area inexpensively. Color choice is more limited than with latex and you can't paint over a coat of portland cement paint without special conditioning.

Application of portland cement paint takes much more time because the surface must be damp when you apply the paint (best done with a large brush, not a roller), and the surface must be kept damp for about 72 hours after application to allow the cement in the paint to "set" rather than dry. Failure to follow this procedure can result in paint that dries into a dusty powder which not only won't hold, but will be tremendously messy.

Chlorinated Rubber-base: For floors, chlorinated rubber-base paints are excellent because they offer good adhesion and resistance to wear and abrasion.

Epoxy: Epoxy paints harden to a tile-like surface. They too offer excellent adhesion and strength in high-traffic areas. They are harder to lay on though, because they usually require special surface preparations and then blending the resin base with a catalyst before applying.

They are also more expensive than the other types mentioned.

Preparation

Proper preparations are the key to successful concrete painting. Take off loose dirt and cement particles with a wire brush. If possible, wash the area with a hose — otherwise scrub and rinse as thoroughly as possible with a sponge. If the surface has a lot of grease and oil on it, wash with hot water and trisodium phosphate. Rinse, let dry, then if it's a floor or steps, vacuum.

If the surface has a lot of white powdery material, called efflorescence, often found on masonry you must remove it since the paint won't stick to it. Mix a solution of three parts water to one part muriatic acid (add the acid slowly to the water), apply with a rag or brush and then rinse thoroughly. Wear gloves and glasses to protect your eyes while working. Paint the surface as soon as possible afterward; otherwise more efflorescence will build up.

If you are painting masonry that has a coat of old paint on it which is in bad condition you must either remove the paint with a wire brush, or sandblast it. Whitewash and calcimine finishes must be sandblasted too, as they will not hold your new paint.

If your old coat of paint is merely chalky, you can either seal it with a conditioner or add a strengthener to the masonry paint you plan to use. If you think your masonry requires special attention discuss the problem with a mason or your paint dealer to make sure you are proceeding correctly.

If your surface is too porous to work paint into and have it look good, then you must mix a cement-and-water slurry the consistency of pancake batter. Add very fine sand if the pores in your surface are extremely large. Thoroughly dampen the surface and apply with a brush making sure to force slurry into all the pores. Let "set" as you would cement by keeping damp for a couple of days.

If your masonry has cracks, you must fill them with ready-mix concrete mixed to a stiff consistency. Dig out the cracks and loose mortar, moisten the cracks, fill with ready-mix and trowel in, filling the crack completely. Smooth the patch and let it "set," keeping it moist for a couple of days.

With the exception of portland cement paint, you can apply concrete paint with a roller that has a ½ or ¾-inch nap. Use a whitewash brush to get at parts that are inaccessible with a roller. Don't be afraid to apply paint generously — most masonry soaks it up quickly. You'll want to see that all pores are filled if possible, so go slowly. When you paint a flat surface, you can simply pour the paint and roll it from the surface. Use the same light, even, criss-cross strokes suggested for walls.

Painting Metal

Metals are the trickiest surfaces to paint because you must be particularly careful about what you put on them. A good primer is the key to success. It's the primer that's going to prevent rust and hold the topcoats. Select a quality primer and you'll avoid a lot of problems. Don't leave a primer uncoated — it won't serve the purpose of a topcoat. Two coats of primer followed by a topcoat give the best protection in areas exposed to weather or moisture.

Different metals have different preparation requirements, so if you're in doubt check below, or ask someone who knows.

Appliances And Cabinets

Appliances like refrigerators and freezers, and enameled metal cabinets in kitchens or bathrooms, can be painted if they no longer look as good as they did originally. Clean the surface with detergent and water, coat with a metal

Each of these metal fixtures has its own particular problems and must be handled differently. Be sure to check preparation and type of paint to use before you paint any metal object.

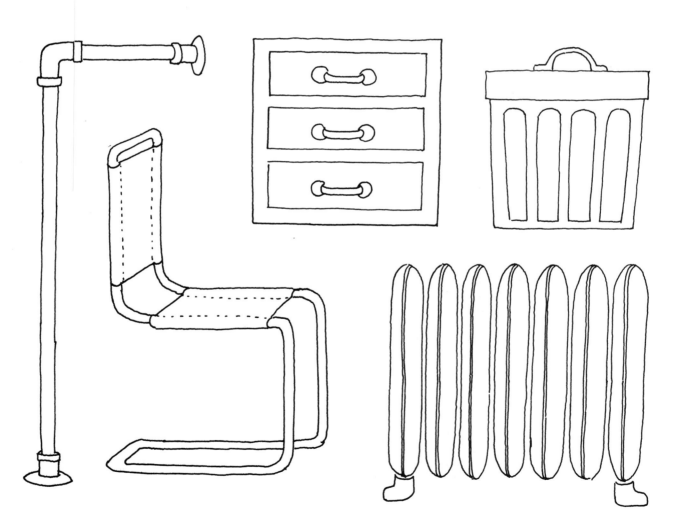

primer and then apply several thin coats of a good quality semi-gloss or satin-finish enamel. Use a small roller to get the smoothest possible surface.

When painting a bathroom medicine chest, be extra careful not to drip paint into the sink while working. If you are unsure of your roller work, metal cabinets and appliances can be spray-painted from a can. Protect all other surfaces around with newspaper and masking (freezer) tape. Either remove knobs, or wrap them with tape. The biggest mistake beginners make is to spray on too thick a coat, which sags and drips. Three very light coats will work much better.

Radiators And Pipes

Radiators and pipes need to be primed with a latex metal sealer or a rust-inhibiting red lead paint before you apply the topcoats. As emphasized in earlier pages, do not paint radiators or heating pipes while they are hot. In the same vein, don't paint pipes that sweat while they are moist. Pipes will hold proper primers and topcoats if applied when the surfaces are at room temperature and absolutely dry.

Other Metal Fixtures

Other steel or iron fixtures you might have — railings, lawn furniture, and so on — should be treated the same way. Sand or brush off all rust and wipe clean, washing with water and detergent if necessary. Coat with a rustproofing primer and then proceed with topcoats.

New downspouts and rain gutters, trash cans and other items made of galvanized iron can be painted with latex or zinc-chloride primers before they receive the topcoats. The surfaces however must be cleaned of the oil coating they usually receive when manufactured. Old galvanized iron that is starting to rust needs to be brushed or sanded, and then coated with a rust-inhibiting primer, the same as you would for a steel surface.

Copper can be painted but you must first remove any of the bluish-green deposit by sanding it lightly by hand. Use a latex primer — one coat will usually do — and then proceed with the topcoats.

New aluminum can simply be wiped and then coated with a latex primer before topcoats are applied. A powdery substance sometimes builds up on older aluminum and must be washed off with water and detergent. Paint with a latex primer and then apply the following coats.

Refinishing Floors

Finishing floors is a task some homeowners shy away from. There's no need to, however, if you obtain the right equipment and plan your work step by step so as not to paint yourself into the proverbial corner.

Before doing any floor work you'll naturally remove all the furniture and rugs. If you do any sanding, remember to remove drapes and shades and even wall decorations, or you'll find them covered with hard-to-remove dust. If it's practical you may even want to remove the baseboard molding for easier sanding close to edges.

Take a good look at your floor. Does it really need refinishing or does it only need a good scrubbing with hot water and a strong detergent (trisodium phosphate mentioned a few pages ago is fine) to get off the wax and crud built up after years of use? You may find that after all, there are very few worn spots and all you need to do after it is clean is lay on another coat of varnish, apply wax, and polish.

Lots of worn spots and nicks, however, call for more attention. Touching them up one by one usually isn't satisfactory because the retouching often shows — you'll have places with light areas, and places with dark areas because of the old and new finishes.

Sanding

It's usually less work in the long run to decide to remove the finish completely. You can do this two ways: by sanding or by brushing on paint remover and scraping, using the process described a few pages back for taking off old paint.

Using a paint remover is a time consuming job and can get expensive. It should only be your course of action if it's impractical to use a big sander — perhaps if your work space is too narrow or inaccessible to a floor sander. In such a case, apply remover and scrape in the direction of the grain of the wood. Remove scrapings, and give surface a light sanding if necessary.

Sanding will probably be your best bet in most cases because it will give you a totally new surface to work with. The sander will actually remove a tiny layer of the wood itself, in addition to the old finish, which will eliminate nicks, gouges and swelling and leave a smooth level surface. Go to a lumber yard or decorating center and rent two sanders: a large floor drum or belt sander for the bulk of the work and a small disk sander for edges, corners, steps and

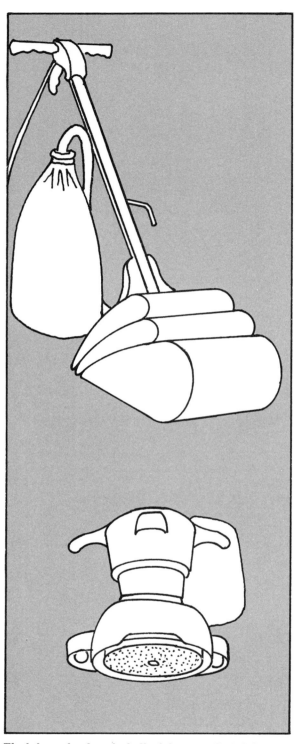

The belt sander does the bulk of the room. Switch from coarse to medium sandpaper after you have finished the diagonal work. A final sanding uses fine sandpaper. A disk sander is used around the edges of a room, and a hand-sander to get into the tightest spots.

other places you can't reach with the large sander. If you have an electric hand sander, this will be useful for catching out-of-the-way areas the disk sander might not reach.

The two sanders aren't difficult to use but you should know certain things about them before you begin. It's important to move the machine constantly, never holding the sander in one spot for any length of time. This will cause oversanding in that spot which will leave a noticeable depression. You can't make up for holes so take pains to avoid them by keeping the machine constantly on the move. When you turn off the machine, keep it moving until it stops to avoid grinding in depressions without realizing it. Since your cord will have a tendency to get in the way, work away from the plug and keep the cord thrown over your shoulder so it won't get underfoot.

The tendency of the large floor sander is to move forward. As you move it, exercise a slight "hold-back" pressure on it so that you can keep it in control. On most machines you can adjust the sanding speed to fit your ability to handle it.

The technique in floor sanding that gives the smoothest results is this: with a coarse-grain sandpaper, begin at a corner and go back and forth sanding diagonally toward the opposite corner. Move the machine in a straight line, never with a circular pattern. Don't worry about the edges now. Overlap your strips by a few inches so as not to leave ridges. Once you've gone over the whole room one way, go over it diagonally in the opposite way, so that you are making an X with the first sanding. Now go over the floor a third time, this time parallel to the boards with a medium-grain sandpaper. You may have to go over it a fourth or fifth time to get the smooth effect you'll want.

Now is the time to attend to the unsanded edges with the smaller disk sander. Begin against the baseboard and work parallel to the wall and then outward to blend the small sander's imprint with that of the larger one. Catch any hard to reach places or spots of finish that remain with an electric hand sander if necessary. In many cases this will be all the sanding required. Vacuum thoroughly and take a good look at your floor. If you are satisfied, you're ready to proceed with the application of the finish. If you see any rough spots or unevenness, go over the whole area again once or twice with a fine grain paper on the large sander. This should do the trick.

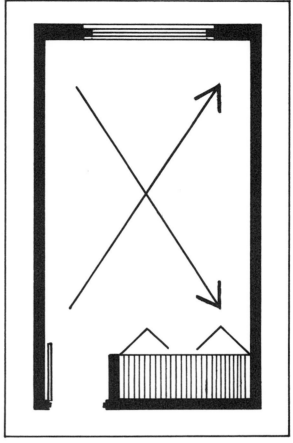

When sanding a floor, begin in a corner and work diagonally to the opposite corner. When you have gone over the whole room this way, begin again in a third corner and work to its opposite, making an X pattern.

Finishing

The next question is what type of finish to apply. There are several from which to choose, including, of course, paint.

Varnish: Varnish provides a tough abrasion-resistant coat, especially if you use a urethane varnish. However, varnishes are difficult to apply because they take so long to dry. Each coat, and you'll probably need three, takes about 24 hours drying time. Because it is slow drying, dust particles are apt to stick to the surface. You'll need to sand lightly between each coat and then wipe away all dust with a rag and turpentine. The first coat should be thinned, one to eight, with a solvent. The topcoats however go on full strength, usually with a brush, and as smoothly as possible.

Varnish will reward patient amateur floor finishers with a marvelously high-gloss sheen if they are willing to take the time needed to do the job right.

Shellac: Shellac is quite a bit less complicated to apply and for this reason is a favorite for floors. It wears well, can be retouched, is comparatively inexpensive and dries quickly. However, it does not have the water resistance that other finishes have, and for this reason it must be carefully waxed for extra protection.

Apply the first coat with a roller or wide brush. Spread thoroughly, taking care not to leave any puddles. Let dry two or three hours. Sand lightly, remove dust, and apply a second coat. Allow it to dry at least three hours. If you add a third coat, give it four to five hours to dry, then sand lightly if necessary, wipe away dust and wax 24 hours later.

Lacquer: Amateurs must take special precautions when finishing with lacquer since it is extremely flammable and the fumes are hazardous to breathe. Make sure you have enough cross ventilation — open doors and wide-open windows are best.

For maple and pine and in some cases oak, you must apply a special lacquer primer — check with your dealer if you are in doubt. After the primer is dry, apply the first coat using a wide brush or roller. Work quickly to avoid lap marks. Allow it to dry an hour or two, sand lightly, dust and then apply the second coat. Let that dry about twelve hours. If it looks like

Always clean up diligently after sanding — sweeping, vacuuming, washing if necessary, so you won't leave any sanding dust that will cause your finish to have a gritty surface.

you'll need another coat, sand the second coat lightly, wipe off dust and apply a third, which should be a mixture of one part recommended thinner to four parts lacquer. You can wax as soon as the lacquer is dry or wait until the surface needs it.

Penetrating Finishes: These give an "in the wood" finish look as opposed to the surface finishes produced by the above. A penetrating finish contains resins which protect by filling the wood pores and then hardening them. They are easy to apply, provide good wear and resistance to water, aren't easily scratched, and can be touched up if necessary.

At most paint stores you can select from a variety of brands that give both clear and stain finishes. To apply you merely brush them on or spread with a rag. Work in an area only as large as you can reach. Apply generously and let soak in for twenty-five to thirty minutes, adding more if it seems to be soaking up quickly. After it has had time to penetrate, wipe off all the excess and then move on to the next work area. Let dry according to directions given on the penetrating-finish can — some dry in a few hours, others should be left overnight — and then give the floor a second coat, proceeding in exactly the same manner. Two coats should do nicely. Wax if you want extra protection.

Stains: For decorating reasons, you may want to stain a floor before applying one of the finishes just discussed. The stain is added right after sanding by brushing it on, waiting a bit and wiping it off. If after wiping you find you want a darker color, apply and wipe a second time. Don't try to obtain a dark hue with one coat. Let dry at least twelve hours before applying your finish coats. Don't use oil-based stains under lacquer or shellac since the lacquer or shellac may dissolve them. Water stains can be used, however.

Paints: Choose either special deck paints (which don't come in many colors) or a good-quality alkyd enamel in a color of your choice. Roll on with a roller, or use a large brush. Allow a good 12 hours between coats. Paint will show wear in heavy traffic areas, but is very attractive in some situations. It can be waxed after a few weeks.

When painting or varnishing floors, apply in sections. Divide the floor into squares that are manageable. Do one area, then move to the next, always working towards an exit.

Spraying

Though spraying on a large scale is not often used in home interiors it is still logical to review the advantages it can offer and go over spraying techniques that are as applicable for use with an aerosol can as they are with a spray-gun rig.

Spraying is efficient for large wall and floor areas that have few openings and few windows and hardware to mask. Spraying equipment is also useful for items from pieces of lawn furniture to fancy room dividers that would be time-consuming to paint with a brush.

Equipment

If the job you're doing is too large for aerosol cans to handle, spray equipment can be rented, or you can purchase gun attachments that fit onto your vacuum cleaner. Follow operating instructions for any spray equipment closely. Precautions are in order when gun spraying: have good ventilation, wear a mask so as not to breathe the fumes, have a fire extinguisher on hand and store flammable paints in safety cans. Stock up plenty of newspapers and a large roll of masking tape to protect surfaces.

Spraying From A Gun

Take a couple of test runs on a disposable surface beforehand, to get the hang of using the gun. Experiment with paint thickness, the distance from the surface, and the motion of your gun and hand.

To begin, point the spray so that it is perpendicular to the surface you are painting — that means you are going to hit it head-on, not at an angle. In most cases this means holding the gun perpendicular too, unless the spray nozzle is tilted. Do not begin by spraying directly at the surface being painted; instead, begin a bit beyond to assure a smooth approach. Try to always hold the gun the same distance from the surface, moving parallel, never swinging back and forth with the wrist as that would cause uneven application. Don't stop in one place while applying or you could cause runs. Overlap strokes to obtain smooth coverage. Do edges, corners, rounded surfaces first, and then go to the broad expanses.

These kitchen cabinets will turn out smoother with a spray than with a roller or brush. The job will be easiest if the doors are removed and propped upright in a convenient area for spraying. The cabinet structure itself is better done with a small roller. To keep sprayed items from sticking, use waxed paper between the object and the newspaper or paint cloth under it.

When spraying outdoors, beware of windy weather. Bugs and dust tend to blow into the paint job and ruin it, or the windblown spray is just too hard to control.

Clean your spray gun by spraying solvent through it right after use or you'll risk paint build-up that's hard to remove. Don't use pins or nails to clear the openings as they may damage them. Instead, use a straw from a broom, or fine wire or a bristle from a hair brush.

Spraying From A Can

You can do a lot of little jobs successfully with canned spray paints. Chairs, small cabinets, tables, trivets and other household items can look like new again, quickly and inexpensively, with a coat or two from an aerosol can.

As with the spray gun equipment, if you observe simple suggestions your work will go much easier. Always shake the can vigorously to allow the paint to mix. Experiment on a piece of cardboard or newspaper first to find the best distance for the smoothest application. Work on newspapers, outside if possible; if not, in a well-ventilated area.

Thoroughly clean the object to be sprayed. Sand if necessary for a smooth surface. On vertical surfaces, hold the can upright, moving the spray back and forth from side to side, always keeping the can the same distance from the object. If you are spraying doors or drawers on a cabinet for instance, open them to be able to cover their edges and the surfaces behind them at the same time. Two or three rapid coats are better than one heavy one. Halting in one spot leaves too much paint in one area and causes runs.

If you must paint a flat surface, hold the can so it is tipped as little as possible but still able to cover the surface. If the object has open areas, such as on grillwork or a trivet, you'll have to tip the can a little to cover the inside edges.

If there's no more paint in the can, recycle your valve. Spraying upside down will clean it out and then you can store it as a spare. Valves can be cleaned with fine wire if they get clogged. Remember that aerosol paints are very flammable and cans should not be stored near any kind of heat. Also, never toss empty cans into an incinerator — you risk an explosion — and never puncture them.

When spray painting (especially metals), try to avoid "orange peeling," which looks like little bumps and is caused by too much paint or too much air pressure from the spray can or gun. Catch orange peeling by wiping off with your hand and respraying.

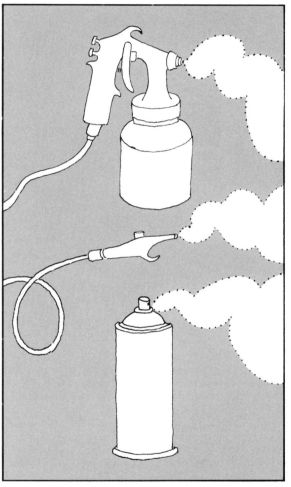

When spraying, hold the can upright to prevent drips. Always maintain the can the same distance from the surface you are covering to prevent uneven thicknesses.

To prevent streaking on large surfaces, overlap strokes and keep the spray moving at all times. Halting in one spot can cause runs.

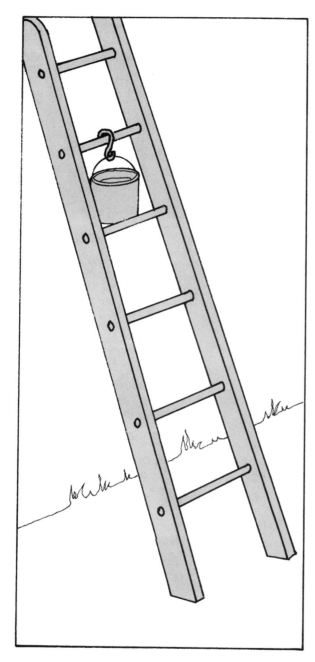

When painting the exterior of your house, start at the top and work down. Affix the bucket to the ladder with an "S" hook. Don't lean out too far past the sides of the ladder. Instead, move it when you can no longer reach easily. Keep your hips between the rails to avoid the possibility of tipping.

Exterior Painting

Any homeowner who does well with a brush or roller on the inside of his or her house needn't be afraid to tackle the exterior. Indeed, many of the methods and suggestions described in the previous pages apply as well to outside painting. All you need do is refer back to them for help. Preparation of masonry and metals is the same for both interior and exterior painting. Wood preparations are generally the same: you will need to clean off peeling or blistering paint, rough up glossy surfaces by sanding, countersink exposed nail heads and fill dents or gouges as you would for interior painting. In addition, you'll have to remove all loose putty or caulking compound and refill in joints, corners and around doors and windows. If your paint has become chalky in appearance, wipe the surface briskly with old towels. If the old paint is in good condition but dirty, wash the walls with detergent and water using a big sponge or broom. Check for loose boards and replace all rotted wood (prime the pieces you'll use as replacements first).

If you know of building defects which allow moisture to seep in behind the walls, remedy them before you paint or you'll have a problem in those places.

Check to see that your gutters are in good repair so that they don't overflow onto your new paint job.

If you are working with new wood, of course you must fill nail holes, clean, sand if necessary and seal with a primer marketed for exterior use.

Plan to paint when the weather is good — it should be above 45 to 50 degrees. Naturally, you won't want to paint when it's windy or the wet paint surfaces will pick up dust and grit. If you've had hard rains and your walls are wet, give them a few sunny days to dry. If you are an early morning person, make sure the dew has evaporated before you begin.

With the exception of a ladder, an S-hook for attaching the bucket, and wide brushes, the equipment you have for interior work will do fine.

Exterior paint isn't the same as that used for interiors. The most commonly used outdoor paint is exterior latex — it's simple to spread, it dries quickly and comes in a variety of colors. You may want to use portland cement paint (see our chapter on concrete) for masonry walls that let moisture in, since it can stop minor seepage. Patios, steps and garage floors can be painted with epoxy concrete enamel for extra resistance to traffic and the elements.

To figure how much paint you need, take the height of the house (add two feet if you have a pitched roof) and multiply it by the distance around the foundation. This will give you the number of square feet of area to be covered. Divide by 500, which is the approximate number of square feet covered by a gallon, and you have the number of gallons you need. A general rule of thumb is to buy one gallon of trim paint (enamel in most cases) unless your house is unusually large with more than the average number of windows and doors.

How many coats will you need? Bare wood needs two coats in addition to the primer coat. If in good condition, previously-painted wood only needs one. If the paint is in bad shape and needs much preparation, or if it's been some years since the house has been painted, you'll probably want to give it two coats.

How do you go about starting? First decide what equipment you'll use. Rollers are difficult to use on some sidings, easy on others. If you use a roller you'll probably want to have a brush to catch places the roller misses as you go. Or you may want to stick with a good wide brush — it'll get you through the job nicely.

Spray equipment covers a lot of area in a little time but may be more difficult for the amateur to use. See our chapter on spraying and then decide.

When you paint a house, you start from the highest point and work down. Some people like to do the trim last, some prefer to do it as they go along to avoid moving the ladder so often. If you paint it at the same time, take with you on the ladder a trim brush, along with the wide brush, rag, and bucket of paint. Place the ladder solidly against the wall. Wearing shoes that won't slip, (caution: sneakers are soft and your feet might get tired from the rungs), climb up and attach the bucket to the ladder with an "S" hook. Keep one hand on the ladder, the other on the brush. Don't reach too far to either side — its much safer to get down and move the ladder. If you have shrubs or plants below you, cover them with a drop cloth or newspapers. Don't let paint drip on windows. In a couple of days you'll have the best looking home on the block!

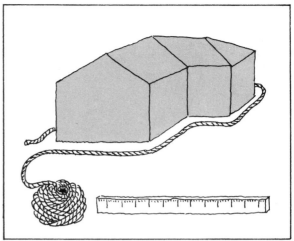

If it seems too hard a job to measure your house with a steel or tape rule, you can always use a ball of string. Wrap the string around the perimeter of the house and cut the total measurement from the ball. Then measure the string you have cut against a yardstick, a 6-foot table or whatever convenient unit you can find. Measuring height is harder, but you can usually estimate it well enough by figuring 10 feet per story.

If you need to use steps before they would be able to dry, either paint every other one or paint one side, then the other.

2
Wallpapering

Few do-it-yourself decorating projects produce as satisfying and rapid a result as wallpapering. In a day, you can change the whole feel of a room and still have the energy to tackle another the next.

As with paints, there have been tremendous improvements in wallpapers over the last fifteen years. So many in fact, that the term wallpaper is now inadequate; wallcovering more appropriately describes the range of materials available. In your dealer's books find vinyl, foil, fabric, cork, burlap, grasspaper, flocked, even wood coverings—all produced by the roll to be applied in the same manner as the traditional pulp wallpapers.

The new wallcoverings offer decorating flexibility with their variety of texture, color, and design. But equally important are the several practical advantages they provide. They have extra strength which means greater ease in hanging and more resistance to scuffs and tears. Most are washable. Some vinyls and foils are steam resistant, and therefore usable in bathrooms and kitchens. Many are strippable—important when you next have the urge to redecorate—and nearly all come pretrimmed which saves you the exasperating job of cutting the selvage edges from each strip prior to hanging. Some are even prepasted which means all you need do is soak the strip in water before hanging.

Choosing The Right Covering

The number of coverings from which you can choose in a large home decorating center is staggering. Indeed, for many choosing an appropriate covering is more time-consuming than getting it on the wall! There are both practical and aesthetic questions to keep in mind as you browse through the sample books.

How durable a covering do you need? Are the walls part of a high-traffic area such as a hallway, a child's room, bathroom, or kitchen? Then spend the extra money for a washable vinyl or fabric-backed covering that's guaranteed to take the wear and tear of greasy hands, cooking splashes, furniture marks, water vapor and so on. If extreme durability isn't required, you can still get extra protection from regular pulp paper by selecting one that has a plastic coating that helps make it soil resistant. Often pulp papers are treated to keep colors from running which allows wiping occasionally with a damp cloth.

Do you need a non-fade covering? Most vinyl and fabric-backed coverings are sunfast, while regular pulp papers tend to fade quickly in direct sunlight.

How difficult to hang is the paper you've chosen? Easiest of course are the no-match coverings such as solid colors, weaves, textures, stripes, and nonmatching prints.

Most matches aren't difficult though, if you vow to take pains before you begin. Success requires accurate measuring of each strip, perfect butting against the previous strip and care taken not to let the strip "stretch" while being hung as some heavier coverings are apt to do. (Stretching can be avoided by applying the strip to the wall as quickly as possible. If a strip does stretch, make your match at eye level, not near the ceiling.) Places where matching is a problem are dormered rooms, and rooms where the walls or ceiling line isn't straight. Best to check

These commonly-accepted visual principles are useful when you're leafing through sample books:

Dark colors tend to make a room seem smaller.

Vertical stripes or strong vertical designs can make a low ceiling appear higher.

Horizontal stripes or strong horizontal patterns can make a narrow room seem wider.

Because of limitations of sample size, papers with bold or large designs tend to be stronger on a wall than they appear in the book. If you're not sure you'll love an audacious print but are willing to gamble the price of a single roll and your time, do this: order enough to complete the job with the condition you may return all but a single roll should you find that the pattern is not for you. (It's not a good idea to buy only one roll. If you like the paper and want to continue, the subsequent rolls ordered may come from another print run and may vary a shade or two from the original.) Hang a few strips, and live with them a day or two to decide whether or not you like the pattern. If you don't, return the unused rolls and choose another pattern. Either strip off or paper over the original strips.

Large patterns can pose matching problems in a room with lots of openings as well as create a broken-up look. Very small patterns may be less striking on a wall than they were in the book.

Consider carefully before hanging a high-gloss vinyl or solid color foil in a room that receives a lot of direct sunlight. The warm glow produced by artificial lighting may be inviting, but full sun can produce an unbearable glare.

Wallcoverings are no longer only papers. Vinyl, fabric, foil, even thin wood and cork are now sold in rolls for pasting on walls.

corners with a string tied to a weight beforehand. Hold the string up at a top corner and let the weight dangle above the floor. The string is straight, and now you can tell how far off the straightness of the corner is. If it's crooked, no match will be perfect, and a scattered print or a small one would make the crookedness appear less conspicuous.

Very heavy papers can be downright unmanageable if you're working alone. If the roll is particularly heavy, the paste-laden strips will be too. Round up help if you're going to be laying on more than a few strips.

What width roll will you be working with? Rolls vary in width from 18 to 54 inches. Many do-it-yourselfers find something in the 26 to 28 inch range a workable compromise. You cover more area and use less effort than with the very narrow rolls, yet you don't have to cope with the weight and awkwardness of a 54-inch strip.

Does the covering you've chosen have a special "quirk?" Tell the dealer you plan to do the work yourself and ask if there are any particular requirements you should know about. By now you are match savvy, but check beyond that. For example, some thin foils require liner papers. (All foils emphasize imperfections in walls, so if the walls you're papering aren't in very good condition, you should choose a different type of covering.) Some flocked prints and grasspapers won't recover from the pasty prints you're bound to leave at some time during the application. Some fragile fabric-backed coverings require special adhesives. Though rare, some papers still don't come pretrimmed. If yours isn't, can it be done by the dealer or will it be your job? Some imported papers even come in sheets instead of rolls. Depending on the particular problem, your skills and dealer advice, it may be less frustrating to toss out your first choice and opt for a less-complicated second. You'll love it just as much, or more, for its simplicity in hanging!

The color and design of your wall coverings are, of course, a matter of personal taste — you'll find no decoratorish dos and don'ts on these pages.

Many dealers are willing either to give you a bit of the sample or let you borrow the book over a weekend. Do this whenever possible so you can hold the sample next to windows, floor, bookcases, curtains, furniture and other elements it will be required to blend with. You'll also want to look at it under artificial and natural lighting.

Small patterns with frequent repeats are easy to match and leave little waste in cutting. Larger designs are not necessarily harder to match, but there will be more waste and people tend to make more mistakes when they cut large patterns, simply because the match is not as apparent from close up.

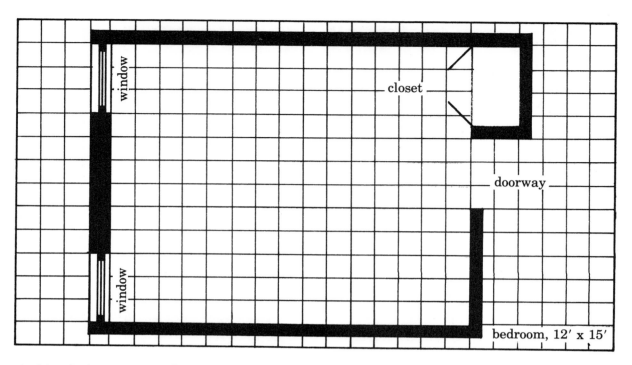

window

window

closet

doorway

bedroom, 12' x 15'

Applying the 4-step measuring formula is easy in rectangular rooms. One caution however, stick closely to the "subtract one roll per two standard openings" rule so you'll be sure to have enough. The arithmetic to use for this room is detailed in the text.

Estimating Quantity

You've picked your pattern. Now how much should you order? Your dealer will talk about "single rolls," a standard unit of measure in the wallcovering trade. The material you've chosen may actually come in a single, double, or triple roll. A single roll of a traditional-width (22-28 inches) covering contains about 36 square feet and covers approximately 30 square feet once waste from match and trim are accounted for. Figuring how many single rolls you need is done with an easy four-step formula. Suppose you have a 12 by 15-foot room with an 8-foot ceiling. It has two windows, one average-size closet and one doorway.

1. Forgetting openings for the moment, obtain the perimeter, which is the distance around

the room. In this case it's 12 + 15 + 12 + 15 = 54 feet.

2. Obtain the total square feet of wall space by multiplying the perimeter (54 feet) by ceiling height, 8 feet: 54 × 8 = 432 square feet.

3. Divide the area in square feet by 30 (the approximate number of square feet in each roll). 432 divided by 30 is 14.4. Round off to the nearest full roll — 15.

4. Deduct one roll for every two average openings such as standard-size windows and doors. (If you have a fireplace that takes up about as much area as a door, count it as an average opening. If you have a double sliding glass door, count it as two, and so on.) In this case, assuming the closet is about the size of a door, you would deduct 2 rolls, for four average openings: one door, two windows, one closet. Consequently, you'd need to order 13 single rolls — or 7 double rolls if that is the only way the paper comes.

If you plan to order paper for a ceiling, the formula for estimating is simple: length times width divided by 30 square feet per roll, rounded off to the nearest whole number will give you the number of single rolls you'll need.

Using the room example above, multiply 15 times 12, which gives you 180 square feet. Dividing that by 30, you'll find you need 6 single rolls for the ceiling.

Ask your dealer to check your estimate. If you have measured, figured closely, and planned to have "just enough," order an extra roll. This will avoid the possibility of having to reorder from a different print run to finish up. It will also give you some extra paper in case you need to repair a strip in the future.

In a room with slanted walls or dormers you'll have extra area to cover that's not included in figuring the perimeter at the baseboard level. Either figure the perimeter at ceiling level to encompass all the jogs which represent additional surface to cover, or figure the square feet at the baseboard as you would normally, then measure and add the square feet that additional area in the dormers represents.

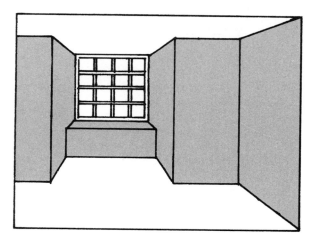

If you have a room with columns, partitions that jut into the room, or recessed areas such as an alcove or bay window, be sure to include them as part of the perimeter when measuring, as each surface represents extra area to be covered.

Equipment

How much equipment you need will depend on the amount of papering you plan to do. If you're going to tackle several rooms, use the traditionally-recommended tools that will speed work in the long run. Most can be bought or rented from a large home decorating center.

If you are only doing a wall or a small room, you might be able to get along with a paste brush, a smoothing brush, a seam roller and shears or a matte knife. All except shears or knife are often sold together in inexpensive wallpapering kits. On the facing page is an ideal equipment checklist that includes all the stray items most people will find they need. In parentheses are workable substitutes for each item, so the list may not present any additional expense.

Being professionally equipped can make for more efficient papering on big jobs. On smaller ones you can make do with some very workable substitutes found around the home. Essential to any "equipment" list is a big stack of newspapers to facilitate pasting.

To avoid adhesion problems it's important to buy the paste recommended for the covering you've chosen. Many heavier coverings need a rugged paste to prevent peeling at the edges. If you're in doubt, seek your dealer's advice.

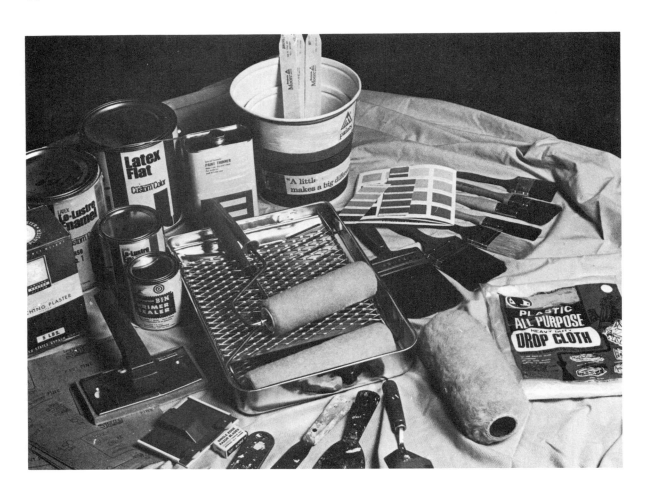

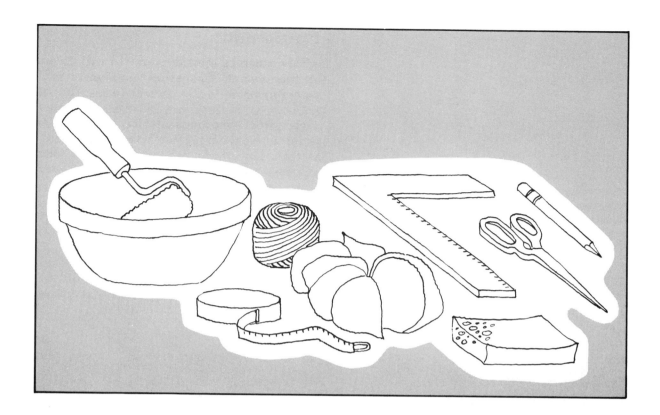

folding paste table or large piece of plywood on sawhorses (kitchen table; two card tables; or if you're athletic, large uncarpeted floor space)

paste brush (paint roller)

paste bucket (dishpan or large bowl or baking pan)

smoothing brush for smoothing paper to wall (a wad of clean rags works well with vinyl and foil coverings)

trimming knife or trimming wheel for cutting paper around windows, doors, and baseboards (single-edge razor blade, sharp matte knife or shears)

tape measure or yardstick, carpenter's square

pencil

seam roller

chalked plumb line (weighted string the height of the wall, which can serve as a guide for making a vertical line)

ladder (reliable stool or chair)

sponge, soft clean rags, plenty of newspaper and a receptacle for used ones

water tray for prepasted wallcoverings (you can also work from a large sink, wash basin or bathtub)

paste: The paste you buy will be determined by the covering you want to hang. Vinyls, foils and fabrics are heavier than pulps and usually require a stronger paste. Strengtheners can be added to paste for extra adhesion if a very heavy covering is being used, or if a particularly glossy surface is being papered. By purchasing your paste where you buy the wallcovering, the dealer can suggest one that's sure to guarantee good adhesion.

Preparations

Before mixing your paste and cutting your first strip, you'll want to prepare the room for papering. If your walls need special treatment, see our special problems section further on. Next, check to see if any part of the room needs painting. If yes, this is the time to do it. Ceilings, borders, moldings, windows, bookshelves and special trims should be painted before papering. (In the rare case that you'll be papering a ceiling, plan to do it before you tackle the walls.)

The Work Station

Smooth set-up of your work station is as important as the papering process itself. Some people find that the "cut and paste" area should be in a room adjacent to that being papered. Others prefer to have as few steps as possible between pasting and hanging operations. Where you locate your work area depends on the size of the room and the available work space.

Two keys to papering sanity are a stable work table (you'll be pasting vigorously after a strip or two) lined with plenty of newspaper (peel off the wet layer after pasting each strip). Some people can manage on the floor, but it does get tiring to crawl so much. If you are a sloppy paster, protect the floor underneath the table with an old sheet or drop cloth. (Newspaper becomes too sticky to be useful.) Paste spatters and drops are easy to remove if you wipe up with a sponge or damp cloth as you go along.

The Room

Next, move lamps and small pieces of furniture out of the room. Group larger pieces away from walls. If necessary you can cover them with drop cloths, but you probably won't have to.

Remove wall decorations and the hooks and nails that hold them. Patch nail holes if necessary. Remove switch plates from electrical fixtures. If removal is too much of a job, simply unscrew them and let them hang. Techniques

A wobbly work area won't do — choose your pasting table with stability in mind. If it is necessary to use two card tables, brace them together with tape or string to avoid their pulling apart and creating a crevice when you're pasting.

Some people find that working on a large floor area simplifies the cutting task. A measured length of floor space or length of wood cut to the desired strip length make good floor cutting guides. If you decide to paste on the floor, be aware that the frequent deep-knee bends will tire you more quickly.

for papering and trimming around them follow in the next section.

The Starting Point

Also a part of the preparations is planning the location of your first strip. If you are hanging a paper that requires no match, such as a weave, stripe, or solid color, plan to hang the first strip at the right or left of a door or large window and work toward the largest area of unbroken wall space.

If your pattern has a dominant design such as large geometric shapes, scenes or symmetrical groupings, it's better to start at a major focal point in the room such as over a mantle, or at the center of a wall area toward which a furniture grouping faces. To avoid ending up with a narrow last strip in a prominent area, take the precaution of "measuring" around the room, marking off roll widths from the place you plan to begin. If you end up with a small strip that will detract from the overall flow of the pattern, try centering a seam at the starting focal point, instead of centering the strip.

Working with a pronounced design also requires thinking about where you want your pattern to start at the ceiling line. Hold up a roll and decide if it looks best if the pattern begins at the ceiling or breaks in the middle.

Once you know where to place the first strip, you need to "plumb" the wall to assure that the strip hangs perfectly straight. Most rooms, especially those in older buildings, aren't "true." Beginning without marking a vertical line may result in a papering job that makes the room look crooked, especially if large-design patterns are used.

Take your chalked plumbline or your substitute and tack it at the ceiling, at the place the free edge of your first strip will be. Hold the chalk line taut at the baseboard and snap it against the wall. Your first strip will be placed along this vertical line. If you have no chalk line, make enough pencil marks along the weighted string you are using to guide you when you put the first strip up.

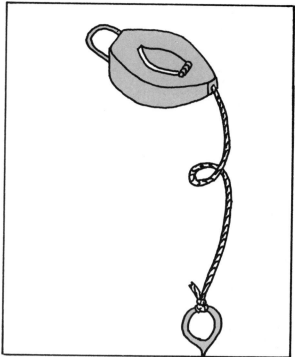

Though it may first appear to be a frivolous extra step, marking a true vertical line with a weighted chalked string is a good idea, absolutely essential if you're working with a pattern. If you don't, you run the risk of crooked strips and ultimately the appearance of a crooked room.

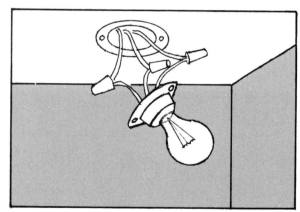

Simply unscrew and let dangle any light fixtures that are too hard to remove. Fitting paper around them is described in the section on trimming.

The young couple shown papering a room on the following pages are still spry enough to set up their work area on the floor. If you have no large table, this may be your only choice.

Matching And Cutting

There are two approaches to cutting: some people like to get it over with in one operation. Others prefer to cut the first two strips, hang them and then proceed to the next which enables you to recheck pattern match each time. Cutting piece-meal is a better bet if your room has several openings.

There are two types of pattern match: set and drop. In set patterns the designs follow each other horizontally. In drop patterns they run "down hill" or diagonally to give relief to the overall look. Most drop patterns today are designed so that the edges are no more a matching problem than set patterns, but if your paper seems difficult, either because it matches diagonally or because the pattern is very large, you may find it easier and less wasteful to work from two rolls, cutting first from one then matching with a strip from the second.

To aid in cutting, mark off on the floor a length the exact height of the wall or cut a strip of molding or a 2 by 4 the required length to use as a measuring guide. When cutting the first strip, add an extra 3 inches at the top and at the bottom. Roll out the second next to the first, line it up to get a match, and cut, again allowing about 3 inches on each end for trim. Chances are your trim allowance on the second strip will be more if your pattern is a drop match or a large pattern. Matching for remaining strips should go smoothly after the first two are cut — but remember not to paste both your strips up before you cut the next piece, since you will always need one handy to match to. It's a good idea with complicated patterns to check the match before cutting each strip.

To take the "curl" out of the strips roll them once or twice in the opposite direction or run them over the edge of your paste table, pattern-side up. You will usually need to do this with pulp papers.

Pasting

If your plumb line is marked and first strips cut, you are ready to prepare the paste and take brush in hand. Be faithful to package directions in mixing your paste, adding the powder to the water to avoid making lumps. Stir to a workable, lumpless consistency. A wire whisk works wonders in dissolving stubborn lumps. If some persist, run paste through cheese cloth or a large-hole sieve, or toss them out as they appear in pasting.

Use a carpenter's square to get your line straight when cutting a strip. Make your line with a pencil and cut along it with scissors unless you are used to cutting paper with a knife.

Running a strip, face-side-up, over the edge of a table will get the "fight" out of its curl.

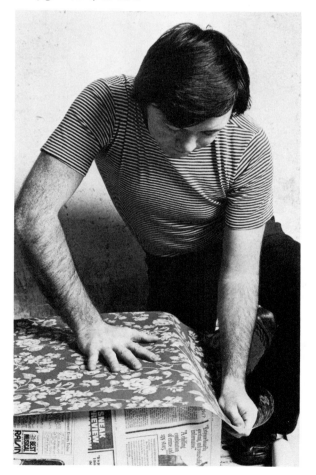

Paste mixed precisely according to package directions should yield the not-too-runny, not-too-thick consistency that offers the best adhesion.

Every couple of strips wipe or sponge off the paste you will have dabbed here and there before it dries. Clean your cutting tools, smoothing brush, and hands from time to time.

Butting seams may not be possible in two instances: on strips that end in corners (or slightly round them) and on the last strip hung — which presumably meets one previously hung. In corners, butting isn't recommended because most rooms aren't perfectly square — you're apt to have the strip rounding the corner by an inch on top, two inches on the bottom. In such a case, trim the strip to match a plumb mark and hang the next one, overlapping the previous strip by ¼ inch or so.

Put the first strip face down on your newspaper-covered work surface. Decide to always put the top at the same end. Using an up-and-down-the-strip motion, paste the top third of the strip. To keep the paste from drying out and to make the strip portable, fold the first section to itself (paste to paste of course) taking care not to crease the fold. Paste the bottom two-thirds of the strip and fold it to itself in the same manner.

Take care to paste evenly, covering the whole strip. Bare spots can appear as blisters once the paste dries. First-timers are apt to miss edges: don't — this can cause peeling problems later on.

Perhaps you've seen professionals paste strips and set them aside before hanging. This process is called "curing" and it allows the paste to uniformly permeate the paper and softens it to give it manageability. Most once-a-year paperhangers work at a sufficiently relaxed pace to allow curing to happen automatically. You can judge for yourself — if the strips seem stiff, let them cure a few minutes before applying.

Two special notes here: remove the paste-marked layer of newspaper after completing each strip until you've got the hang of on-target pasting. (Many of us don't ever reach that stage, finding it more efficient to splash away and then juggle newspapers to begin with a dry surface each time.) Keep a damp rag in a bucket nearby for wiping hands from time to time. This will save your sanity — as well as the face of your paper as you fold, carry, and apply strips. (Be especially paste-splotch conscious if you are working with flocked material or grasspaper.)

Many coverings come prepasted which means you simply add the water. Strips are cut, rolled pasted-side out, and soaked separately for a prescribed time (usually less than a minute) in a waterbox. You can apply it to the wall directly from the waterbox. Take the top of the strip, gradually unroll it, moving up the stool or ladder at the same time. Once the strip is hung, move the waterbox under the location of the next strip.

Prepasted paper can save work if you make absolutely certain that the paste on each strip is completely wet. If adhesion looks and feels less than perfect, you need to take more pains with the wetting process. Some professional paperhangers pay no attention to the waterbox, preferring instead to cover each strip with a thinner paste mixture to guarantee adhesion. Some wall conditions may even require this. If you are in doubt, ask your dealer for advice, or test one strip. After it dries you'll be able to determine whether you'll need to add strength with a paste coat of your own.

Brush the length of the strips, taking special care not to miss any of the edges. If you meet up with lumps while brushing on the paste, remove them from the strips.

Folding the paper over on itself in the manner shown not only makes it easier to carry, it assures that the paste won't dry out as you let the paper cure. Take care not to crease the folds.

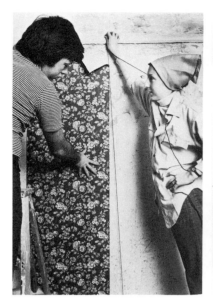 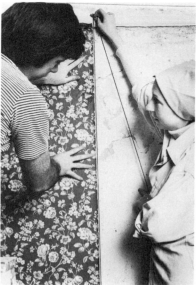 

If you get a bad start like the one above, simply take the strip by the top corners, pull off gently and then reapply, lining up the edge with the plumbline. If you're only off a hair, the strip can be positioned on the wall using flattened hands to apply more equal pressure to the strip.

Once the strip is in position at the top, you are ready to unfold the bottom section which should line up easily with your plumb mark.

When the strip is firmly on the wall, go over it with your smoothing brush, smoothing first the length of the strip, then back and forth to assure that the edges are firmly pressed to the surface

Hanging

After a strip or two, papering will cease to be the awkward process it first seems to be, though in this case, two people are often better than one. The first strip, remember, must line up with your plumb mark. Stand on your ladder, unfold the top third of the strip, holding it by the corners. Taking care not to let it sway, place it at the top of the wall, leaving about 3 inches for trim overlapping the ceiling. Gently line up the top third with the plumb mark. Give the top a light brushing with the smoothing brush to hold it to the wall, and then step back to check position. If you need to adjust, do it with a sliding motion using the palms of your hands. Take care not to tear the more fragile pulp papers. Once your strip is lined up, brush down the top part, unfold the rest of the strip and gently apply it to the wall from the top down, brushing lightly as you go. If you should lose your grip and the strip plops crookedly against the wall, don't panic. Hold the bottom corners, gently pull it away, and reapply.

Check the whole strip for position and then go over it with the smoothing brush, stroking up or down the middle and then back and forth to the edges.

Be particularly careful to smooth out air bubbles. Heavy coverings have a tendency to trap more air than lighter coverings. If bubbles show up afterward, you will have to prick them with a pin and shoot paste behind them with a hypodermic needle — a painstaking process, so vow to paste and smooth conscientiously.

The next strip goes up in the same manner. Line up a perfect match and butt the edges together to make a seam. Butt as tightly as possible since some coverings contract when they dry and a loose seam will be even more obvious. The heavy papers are easy to butt because of their strength. Be cautious with pulp papers though, since vigorous attempts to make the edges meet can tear your paper.

Trimming

Ceiling And Baseboard

To trim overage, simply crease the paper at the ceiling, baseboard, or around door and window casings with the back of your shears or your fingers, nail sides down. If your paper is fragile and you are afraid of tearing it, fit and crease by tapping the paper gently into the corner with your smoothing brush. Cut along the crease with a razor blade, matte knife or trimming wheel, or pull the paper away from the wall, cut along the crease with shears and then replace. Dull knives will tear wet paper, so if your knife isn't in top condition, let the paper dry a little before triming. The best trimming tool for any area is the one that's easiest for you to handle. If you have fancy shaped woodwork such as the angles found under windowsills to trim around, try using a putty knife as a cutting guide.

When you get to a corner, crease the paper with your fingernails or some other not-too-sharp instrument like the back of a scissors. If the paper needs to be trimmed to fit over the baseboard, at the ceiling line or along a door or window frame, you can pull the paper out from the wall a bit and cut along the crease with scissors. Another method is to use a trimming wheel, or to let the paper dry a bit, and cut it with a matte knife.

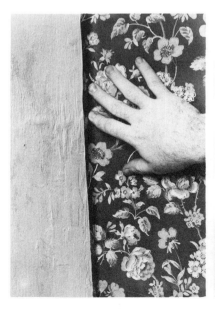  

To trim around a window frame, first make a diagonal cut from the edge of the strip upwards to the top corner of the frame.

Continue to apply the paper, creasing the excess out of your way as you go. As you near the bottom of the window frame, make another diagonal cut, this time downwards from the edge of the strip to meet the bottom corner of the frame.

After the paper is smoothed and creased well into the corners, trim excess as usual.

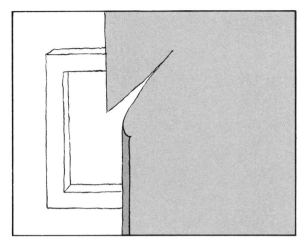

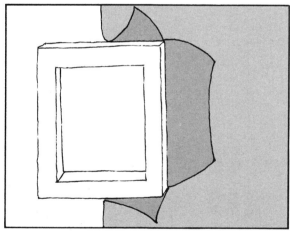

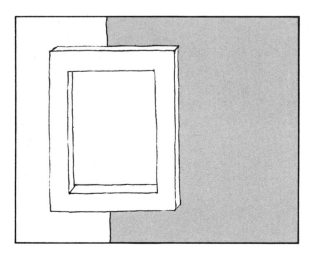

Window And Door Frames

You can cope with most window and door frames easily by cutting the paper to fit around them right on the wall. Begin as you would ordinarily, at the ceiling, applying, matching and butting. When you reach the place where the paper touches a corner of the casing, make a diagonal cut from the edge of the strip upwards to where it touches the top corner of the casing. This will allow you to finish placing the strip down the side of the window or door, bending the extra paper out of your way as you go. Do the same at the bottom corner if you are fitting around a window. Trim the excess as usual around the frame.

Switches And Wall Plugs

Trimming around open switch boxes and wall plugs is an easy task. Apply the strip normally, covering the open switch or plug area. When the strip has been smoothed, trim away paper with a razor blade. Some people find that cutting a small X over the switch area, peeling back the tips, and then snipping off each point is a good way to avoid trimming off too much. You don't want to trim to fit the plate exactly; plan to leave a third of an inch or so. Use the plate as a guide if necessary.

Jutting Fixtures

Small, jutting wall fixtures like side lamps and thermostats that can't be removed can be trimmed much like a window frame. Apply the paper up to the obstacle, then pierce the paper directly over the object and cut an X. The flaps of the X will open out, allowing you to continue applying the paper around the fixture. The flaps are trimmed after smoothing.

If the fixture is large, like a medicine cabinet, you can either handle it like a window, or you can measure and cut the entire strip vertically so that the two pieces can be applied alongside the fixture and then rejoined by butting once you've passed the fixture. Or you can leave the strip whole above the fixture, cut up from the bottom just far enough to accomodate it, then join the cut below it. The latter method is the more professional looking if you can manage it.

Some people have devised a third way. They measure the fixture — a bathroom wall cabinet, say — and draw onto the back of the paper where it will fall. They then cut out this area leaving an inch or so to trim, also making diagonal cuts at the corners, and then cut vertically up to the area from the bottom of the strip.

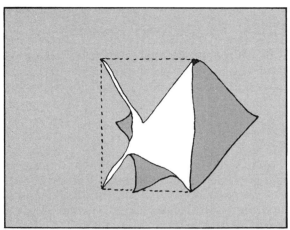

Fit and trim around small jutting fixtures like thermostats with the X method. Small embroidery scissors are helpful here to pierce the paper over the center of the fixture and cut neatly to reach each corner accurately. The excess flaps are trimmed off entirely.

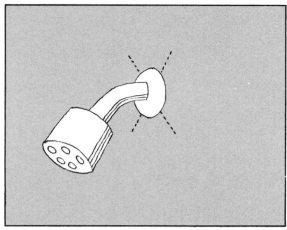

If a jutting fixture requires a large X hole to get it through the paper (a shower head, for instance), you may not be able to trim off the flaps of the X entirely and still cover the hole with the base of the fixture. If the slits are neat, however, the seams won't show when they are butted and rolled.

To hang a strip over a wall fixture that you've left dangling, begin as you would normally, at the ceiling. When you get to the spot where the fixture is usually bolted, make an X cut just large enough to pull the fixture through. Paste down tips made by the X, trimming where necessary.

If you're good at measuring, this method makes the strip easier to handle.

Since many of the heavier coverings can be used around a tub or shower, you may find yourself fitting around faucets or a shower head. The best way to do it is with the X method described for fitting around small jutting fixtures. Remove the faucet or head plates. Make the X cut in the paper only big enough to be able to pass the fixture through. Paste down as much as possible around the fixture by seaming the X cuts, trim excess and replace plate. It's a good idea to use a silicone sealer at the point the plate edge meets the covering.

If you are dealing with light fixtures that can't be removed, unscrew them and let them dangle before you start to paper. To paper around them, use the X method, cutting the crossing slits large enough to pull the dangling fixture through. In this case, you won't be trimming the flaps off entirely, but only to the base of the fixture. The remainders of the flaps are simply butted like any other seam, and will barely show.

Rolling The Seams

Rolling the seams comes after the trimming operation. Seams are rolled to reinforce adhesion. The best time to do this is after the paste has begun to dry. To know when to roll, experiment with an out-of-the-way seam. If paste squishes out, it's still too wet. Wipe the excess, and wait a bit longer to try again.

Some people just tear out a bit of the paper that falls over a switch box before replacing the plate. Cutting is neater. Care must be taken when using foil papers that no foil is in contact with wiring, as a short circuit can result.

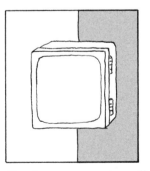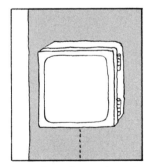

How to paper around a wall cabinet depends on where the seams happen to fall. If the far edge of the strips falls to the other side of the cabinet, you may prefer to cut a center seam only below (or only above) the cabinet. To do this, cut the center seam first, then cut four diagonals from a point in the center of the cabinet outwards to each of the cabinet corners. Butt the center seam below the cabinet, smooth, crease and trim excess.

If the strip falls so that its seam would normally be somewhere near the center of the cabinet, fit and trim as you would a window.

Hard-To-Paper Places

Some rooms, by virtue of their shape, or hard-to-work-in areas like shelves or behind pipes, may present special problems. Let's look at the most common.

Tight Spots

Pipes: Arrange if at all possible for a whole strip to go behind pipes, since trying to butt and roll seams behind them can discourage the most energetic amateur. Of course this means special juggling of the whole strip — with pipes between you and your work surface — but it's the simplest approach.

Radiators: Radiators are tricky, and hot radiators impossible, to work around. If a room containing them is on your papering agenda, plan to do it when the heat is off. In most cases you'll end up butting seams behind radiators but this will be easy if you've got a perfect start above them. If you can't get your hand and smoothing brush behind them, try a paint roller with an extension. If that won't work, use a yardstick or broomhandle wrapped with a clean rag.

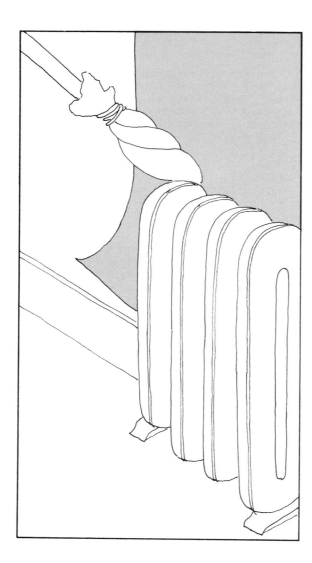

Bookshelves: If removing the shelves is impossible, resign yourself to a piecemeal "cut and fit" job. Make life easier for yourself by using a no-match pattern. Since books are decorative in themselves you'll be happier with a calm background anyway.

Problem Corners

Some corners are inconspicuous because of their location or the furniture, windows or fixtures in them. If you need to, forego perfect match in these to guarantee it in corners which are in the limelight. In some rooms you may have an "outside corner" (one that sticks out) caused by a partition or closet. It's important not only to strive for perfect match on an outside corner but to plan your strips so that the design breaks pleasingly on the corner itself. A geometric design, for instance, wouldn't look well if a fourth of it were on one side of the angle and three-fourths on the other. Try starting your first strip here, and check whether that hurts somewhere else. If there always seems to be something that won't come out right, you'll just have to choose the least annoying solution.

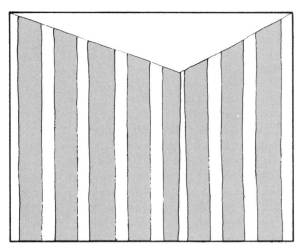

A vertical stripe is a disaster if your corners are slanted. If you have this problem (check with a plumb bob) choose textured papers, scattered patterns, large patterns or horizontal ones.

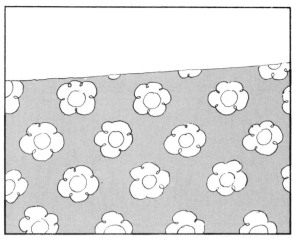

The vertical stripe would have been no problem on this slanted ceiling, but a horizontal pattern looks terrible. Again the only solution is to watch out for these problems before you're stuck with the wrong paper.

Corners are rarely perfectly straight so don't count on getting a perfect butt on an inside corner. Instead, work for a slight overlap which will hardly be noticeable once you've gone over it with a seam roller.

Slanted Walls And Dormers: First determine whether you consider the slanted area as part of the wall or part of the ceiling. If the slant is near the ceiling, you'll probably want to paint it the same color as the ceiling. If the slant ends 3 to 4 feet from the floor you'll probably want to paper it as part of the wall. If the room is such that the whole wall slants at one point, papering will be no problem. If a slanted section juts down from a normal ceiling resulting in triangular sections to paper, matching will be impossible. Do the best you can, by choosing a scattered or small pattern in the first place, or covering mismatches with corner molding painted a tone that matches the background or blends with the pattern.

If you have dormers, you'll probably want to paint the ceilings and paper the walls. As with slanted ceilings, dormers make mismatches inevitable at some point. Remember that when making a matching choice, try to match the inside corners since the mismatches will be less apparent on the outside corners.

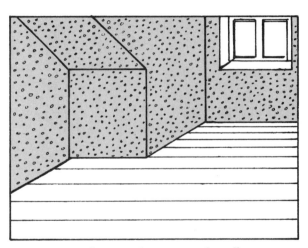

Next-to-no-match scattered patterns and small, easy-to-match patterns like this polka dot are your best bet for rooms with dormers in which no real match is possible where the vertical inside dormer walls meet the slanted walls to either side. The inside corners around the window itself are not a problem.

Accurate measurement and cutting are the only special tricks for papering inside bookshelves. Avoid using papers requiring a match for bookshelf background.

To work alone, you will have to set up a plank platform between two stepladders. Unless the ceiling you're papering is very small, we recommend finding a helper.

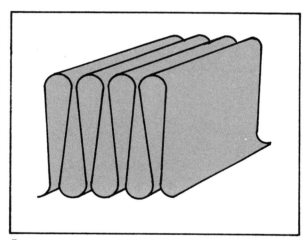

Because strips will be so long, you'll have to fold them ribbon-candy fashion to paper a ceiling.

It's best to paper a ceiling with a partner; one holds the strips, the other applies and smooths, papering the width, not length. The person holding should help check to see that strips are lined up at seams as well as butted. Plan a couple of breaks while ceiling papering. It's an exasperating job and you'll need them.

Ceilings

Papering a ceiling is a much more difficult job than papering walls. Success isn't impossible though if you follow two simple rules: plan to get the ceiling done before the walls, and plan to paper the width of the ceiling not the length, in order to work with the shortest possible strips.

Using a ruler and a roll of paper, very accurately mark off a line the width of the roll parallel to the wall which will be your starting point. Measure the room width in several places to make certain that in case the room isn't square, you'll be cutting strips long enough to fit the maximum width. Add 3 to 4 inches to the ceiling measurement for trim and, as with walls, allow more if a match is necessary.

For the papering process, get a partner if possible — one applies as the other holds. If you plan to tackle it single-handedly, set up two step ladders connected with a plank strong enough to walk on and long enough to provide a platform for pasting the whole strip without getting down to move the ladders. You may want to affix a small platform on top of one or both of the ladders for resting the smoothing brush or paper.

Cut and paste the first strip and fold ribbon-candy fashion for manageability while on the ladder. Leaving 1 inch overlap, apply the top end of the strip to your starting point, supporting the still folded portions with a roll of newspaper covered with a clean rag. Once the first portion is lined up, smooth with your brush and continue to apply, one fold at a time.

Fit and trim around light fixtures with the X method described for switch plates and wall fixtures. Crease and trim surplus on the ends and begin the next strip, butting edges on the first fold as perfectly as possible to assure a smooth seam all across the ceiling.

Match patterns the same way you would on a wall. Remember that many patterns cannot be applied up one wall, across a ceiling and down another because the design would then end upside down on the opposite wall.

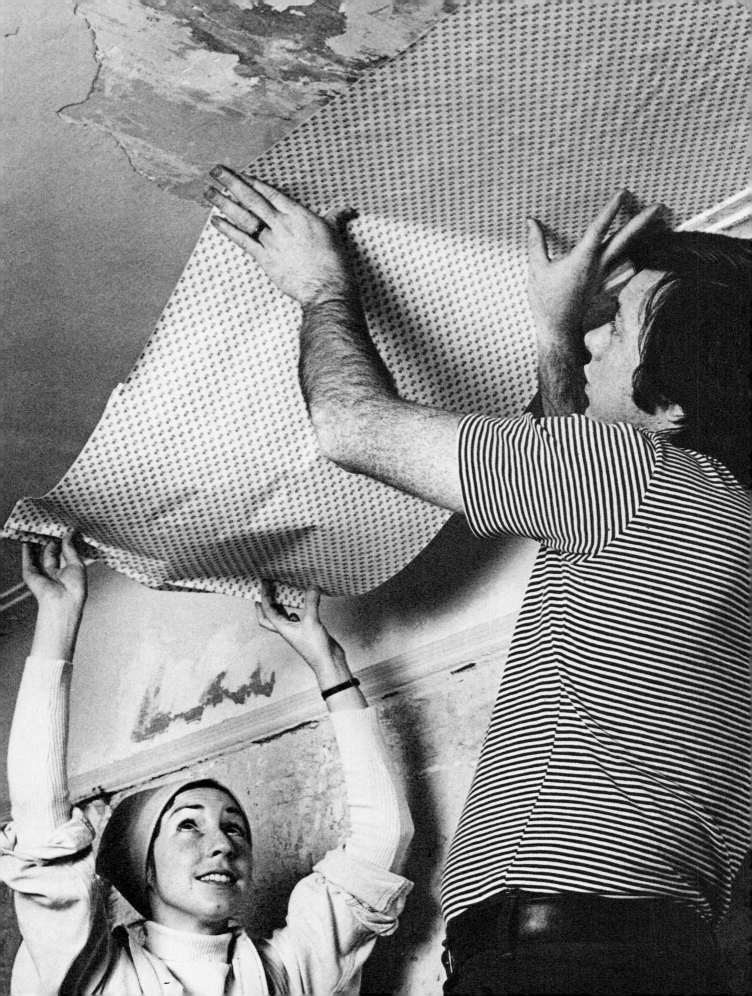

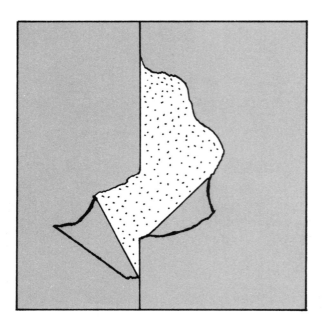

Peeling or crinkling wallpaper such as this has to be taken care of before repapering. If previous paper holds in most places with peeling here and there, remove loose pieces and smooth around the edges with a sander. If the wall is worse, the paper must be removed entirely by soaking and scraping, or with wall steaming equipment. Either method is an arduous but necessary task.

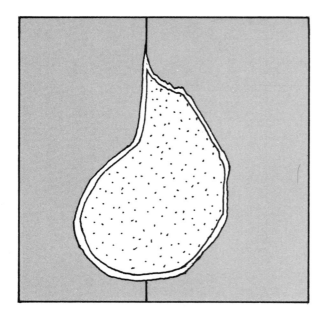

Special Problems

Old Paper

Do you plan to paper a room that's been papered before and wonder if the paper should be removed? If there are two or even three layers, most of which still adhere tightly (they shouldn't peel, crinkle, or lift), you may paper over them. If there are only a few rough spots, remove the loose pieces and sand around them.

If much of the paper is peeling or if there are several layers, plan to remove all of it. This can be done in two ways: buy wallpaper remover and, following package directions closely, soak and then carefully scrape off the layers using a spatula or putty knife. If you have a large area to do, a more efficient way is to rent wall steaming equipment. Most large wallcovering dealers have them.

If your previous paper is one of the strippable vinyls or foils, remove it even though there is only one coat — the surface may be too smooth for good adhesion.

Paint

Most painted walls are fine for papering if they are in good shape. High-gloss enamels however can spell trouble since they too cut down on adhesion. You can either give the walls a once-over with a sander or apply a deglosser which can be purchased at most paint stores. Have adequate ventilation when spreading the deglosser.

Peeling paint needs to be sanded down to a smooth surface before paper is applied.

It's a good idea to scrub painted walls with a detergent to remove grease and oil before papering.

New Walls

New walls that have been plaster "cured" and "sized" are no problem. If they haven't been coated with "wall size," you must apply it before papering. Wall size seals pores on new surfaces.

Sheetrock or plasterboard walls need to be painted with an oil-base wall primer before they are papered. Not only does the primer help adhesion, you won't run the risk of destroying the walls if you should ever want to remove the paper.

Damaged Walls

Cracks in plaster or gouges in wallboard will show if they are not repaired. If you use a vinyl paste for patching you can paper over it immediately. Standard patching plaster requires more time to dry and in addition, you'll need to brush on a coat of shellac to avoid "hot spots" caused by the plaster's alkalinity. The shellac seals off the hot spots which may cause stains or color changes in the paper.

Another way to treat old walls is to apply lining paper. It has no pattern and is inexpensive. Apply as an undercoat to strengthen walls and give a smoother look.

A filler mixture made of 1 pound of wall size, ½ pound of plaster of paris and roughly 5 to 6 quarts of water, applied with a large brush, can do much to smooth the surface of a badly-damaged wall.

Damaged areas such as this need work before they can be papered. There are three methods. Which you use depends on how widespread the damage is. Isolated areas can be patched with plaster, sanded, and sealed with shellac. Large damaged areas can either be covered with a special lining paper to give a smooth surface, or smoothed with a brushed-on coat of the filler mixture described in the text.

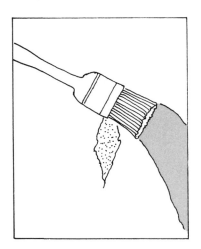

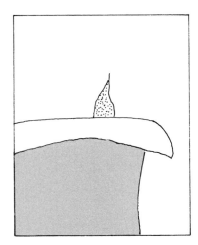

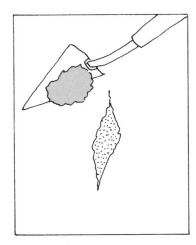

Index